THE SPIRIT OF
THE WILDERNESS

THE SPIRIT OF
THE WILDERNESS

BY

JAMES W. KIMBALL

Photographs by the Author

Jacket Photograph by Les Blacklock

Publishers

T. S. DENISON & COMPANY, INC.

Minneapolis

Contents

DEDICATED TO

My inspiration, my right arm, my companion, my wife—

EMMY LOU KIMBALL

Preface

This book is a series of short essays and true stories written over a period of several years. It has a purpose in striving to bring pleasure and an understanding of the natural world we live in.

But while this book has purpose it has little order or arrangement. If it has a design, that design is for random reading. It was written in many moods and it is hoped the reader will choose and read according to his moods.

While these essays and stories were written for adult readers, each was written with a hope for appeal to youth. To the delight of the author, many have been used in classrooms. Should this book find its way into schools, the author's dream would be fulfilled. The reason is best explained in the following essay which might be titled, "The Spirit of the Wilderness" or simply "Dear Kids."

PART I

Wildlife and Conservation

Kids

Dear Kids

This is a story for the important people—the very young. It is a letter to fourth graders and to those who look much older but have been blessed with the remarkable ability to continue to think with stars in their eyes and to retain that remarkable philosophy of youth in which all the earth is new, wonderful and exciting. It is written to those who see winter's first snow or the unfolding of a leaf in spring as though it were something so new and wonderful that it was happening for the first time.

No one gets more interesting mail than I do. Letters from busy executives, administrators and officials prove that the delicate, sensitive nature of man has been neither smothered nor crushed by the turmoil of 20th-century living. Sportsmen, in their letters, make it clear that they will make whatever sacrifice or do any battle necessary to preserve for posterity the hunting and fishing which is among man's oldest and noblest forms of recreation. Letters from carpenters, housewives, laborers and doctors convince that a trek into the wilderness, even though it be vicariously, refreshes the mind and restores the soul.

Perhaps the best letters of all are from boys and girls—not the ones that say, "I have to write a theme for teacher. Please tell me everything about conservation"— but the sensitive expressive letters of youth which say what they like and how they feel. These are the critics who speak from the heart and strengthen our determination to write the language which they understand. One of the most complimentary letters I ever received was from a cynical man who tried to be critical by saying, "I don't read your stuff much but my kid reads it all the time." Hallelujah!

I received 24 letters from 3rd and 4th graders at the Minnehaha School in Minneapolis. Here is the answer to them and to all who have

David Kimball and his dog

retained the wholesome 4th grade philosophy and stars in their eyes.

Dear Kids,

I have read each of your letters a couple of times. Of all the letters I received, yours were the best because you told me what you liked and how you felt when you read my articles. Because you are young you feel things very keenly and express yourselves most honestly. Sometimes when we get older this is hard for us to do. So you see, your letters tell me not only what you like but what everyone likes and this teaches me how to write better.

Your teacher is helping you learn about the outdoors, wild things, nature and the wilderness. Learning these things will give you pleasure all your lives. You can never be lonely because you can always go and visit with your friend, Nature.

You do not need to go off alone in wild country and live in a tent to enjoy the wilderness because the spirit of the wilderness can be found

A boy finds the spirit of wilderness in a turtle.

in any little spot where things grow wild. You can find the spirit of the wilderness on the edge of a little creek, beside an oak tree in the pasture, in a spider web, listening to a robin's song or even peering into the delicate petals of a flower. You can hear the spirit of the wilderness when the thunder rolls, the wind blows through the trees or when frogs sing in a marsh. You can smell the wilderness in a pine woods or after the lightning flashes or when the air is very clean after a rain.

Once you learn how to look for the spirit of the wilderness, you will find it everywhere, and the people with you who have not learned to look won't even know it is there.

I am glad you liked my stories because I am writing mostly to you. You are the most important people because in just a few years the earth will be yours to care for. I hope you understand it better and treat it more kindly than we have.

Sometimes we have been cruel to our world. We have dumped sewage and chemicals into her waters, burned her forests, drained many of her lakes and marshes, changed her beautiful rivers into ugly ditches and cluttered her landscape with junk, old automobiles and telephone lines.

When we misuse our world she becomes very angry and punishes us. When we treat her kindly she gives us everything we need, but when we foolishly plow up prairie grass she bleeds her life-giving soil into the rivers or lets it be blown away by the wind. When we pollute her lakes and rivers she takes her fish from us and when we destroy the trees, plants and marshes she punishes us by taking away the birds, rabbits, ducks, deer and foxes and leaves us with a bare and ugly landscape to look at.

But even though our world punishes us when we hurt her she doesn't stay angry very long. With a little understanding, kindness and nursing her bruises heal quickly and she gives us back the beauty that she has taken away.

It is still a really good world you are going to inherit, but it needs to be loved and cared for. Keep it beautiful and save a little of it as the true wilderness where sometimes men and women can go and be alone, because now and then the most beautiful experience you can have is being alone.

The Birch-Bark Canoe

The twenty-five-foot-long birch-bark voyageur freighter canoe proudly exhibited by the U. S. Forest Service at their new Voyageur Visitor Center at Ely, Minnesota, was not made by Indians. It has a far more interesting history. After searching the Canadian border from Maine to Minnesota for Indians to make the historic craft, they found the one man who could do it—a scholarly gentleman with a fourth grade education—a determined perfectionist. Where did they find him? On the Big Fork River near the town of Big Fork, Minnesota.

Building authentic Indian birch-bark canoes might well be a lost art had it not been for a fortunate combination of circumstances.

Forty-four years ago William Hafeman was out of a job in Neenah, Wisconsin. His young wife had visited Wirt, Minnesota, when she was thirteen, liked it and suggested they move to northern Minnesota and "live off the country." This appealed to her adventure-loving husband so they moved to Big Fork and have been there ever since. And "live off the country" is exactly what they did.

In spring they made maple syrup, then gathered mushrooms and dried or canned them. Next came berry-picking time. At first Bill Hafeman didn't have a gun but picked off a few grouse with his bow and arrows. When he got a gun, grouse, ducks and deer became important sources of food. Rough fish were netted and smoked and, of course, game fish were often on the menu. For the little cash needed, Bill ran his trap lines. He still does, and, though he is now 66 years old, few men in the community think they could keep up with the wiry gentleman when he takes to the woods on a pair of snowshoes.

A 25-foot birch-bark canoe lies in front of log cabin as Hafeman looks out over river.

Then neighbors came, as neighbors did in those days, and helped the Hafemans build a log cabin on the Big Fork River where Bill had bought seven acres of land for one hundred dollars. The cabin had to be torn down a few years ago to make room for a new road and the Hafemans now live in a pleasant new home. Does Mrs. Hafeman like it better? "It's nice," she said, "and easier to keep clean, but no, the old log cabin was home. I wish they had just moved it over here."

But the old logs from the cabin were not wasted. Bill loves kids and he believes they should have an opportunity to savor their own history. So he took the old logs and built an authentic old log cabin on the river where Scouts and other youth groups are welcome to pull in with their canoes, cook on the old stove and spend the night.

In the old days the Hafemans didn't mind the six-mile walk to town, but from the beginning Bill was determined to make a canoe so he could make the trip via the Big Fork River, a distance of twelve miles.

His first canoe was made of elm bark, and their maiden voyage downstream went pretty well. But returning against the current, the rough-sided craft offered so much resistance that it took them two days to get back.

Then Hafeman met Fred McLean, now in his 80s. Some 50 years ago McLean had been paddling across one of the larger lakes and became stranded on an island because of high winds. A group of Indians were on the island building birch-bark canoes. McLean watched and remembered every detail.

McLean had never built a birch-bark canoe. Hafeman had often tried and failed. It was the keen observations and memory of McLean and the skill of Hafeman which combined to preserve the ancient art of canoe building.

It is no wonder that Hafeman did not work it out for himself because birch-bark canoes are built just the opposite of conventional boats. You don't build them from the inside out, working with the boat upside down over a form. You build them right side up from the outside in.

First, the birch bark, which Hafeman now gets from logging operations, is sewed into a blanket, using the peeled and split roots of spruce trees for thread. With the white surface, outer bark up, to form the inside rather than the outside of the canoe as one would expect, the birch blanket is fitted inside of stakes which have been driven into the ground to form the proper shape of the canoe. The ends are folded and sewed with spruce-root thread. Cedar gunwales are lashed on with more spruce roots, and cedar strips split to $\frac{1}{8}$-inch thickness form the planking. Then, cedar ribs are inserted and pressed up under the gunwales. The final operation is sealing the seams with spruce resin which has been mixed with finely ground charcoal.

The first canoe Hafeman sold was out of real necessity. During the depression of the early '30s, he was working on a "made work" project for $1 a day. The men working with him decided to strike for higher wages. Much as Hafeman needed the money, this seemed ridiculous so he quit rather than strike, cut down a birch tree, made a canoe and sold it for $25.

He has made birch-bark canoes ever since. Now they sell for $175. He also makes a six-foot authentic model for $25. He said, "With nothing more than a knife and an ax, I can go into the woods and build a canoe."

Most of the canoes he sells go to summer homes for their picturesque value as well as their serviceability. Properly maintained, Hafeman believes a birch-bark canoe will last a lifetime. But the seams do need to be touched up occasionally with a torch or a hot iron.

Before making the 25-foot-long canoe for the Forest Service, for which he was paid $1,000, Hafeman studied "The Voyageur's Highway" by Grace Nute, the history of Radisson, and notes from the Hudson's Bay Company. He also studied the remains of old canoes wherever they could be found. Now he has completed a second 25-foot canoe which he says he may or may not sell. He likes to have it around.

Hafeman is also an artist. He could probably make quite a bit of money at it if he didn't prefer spending his time hunting, fishing, guiding hunters and building canoes. His art career started when, at the age of thirteen, he accompanied his mother to the grocery store. There a lightning artist was splashing out paintings which were given to good customers. It looked easy, so young Hafeman borrowed some of his father's white lead and his mother's black sash paint and went to work. A teacher saw the results and was sufficiently impressed to give him six colors in oil. "Within a week," he said, "I was producing paintings on the cardboard from cereal boxes and selling them for $1 apiece. Now his quite remarkable paintings of nature scenes sell for $25 and there is a waiting list of customers.

Hafeman agrees that he could make more money painting, but money doesn't seem to be very important. The most he has ever averaged is $5 a day trapping, and he builds only two or three birch-bark canoes a year. "But," he said, "when I get started on something I can't stop until I believe it is perfected. Now that I have built the biggest birch-bark canoes and believe they are true replicas of those built by the Indians, I may spend a little more time painting."

The Hafemans are obviously living a full and happy life but not just because they have achieved their goal of living off the country. Many men have done this. But few of us can be totally content with simply making a living. The greater reward springs from the knowledge that you have produced something of lasting value—contributed something to the future enlightenment or enjoyment of men.

Whether or not Hafeman's paintings will live I am incompetent to judge. But preservation of the intricate art of building birch-bark canoes which must have been worked out by generations of Indians is a contribution of which any man could be justly proud.

From Longfellow's "The Song of Hiawatha"

> Thus the Birch Canoe Was Builded
> In the valley, by the river,
> In the bosom of the forest;
> And the forest's life was in it,
> All its mystery and its magic,
> All the lightness of the birch-tree,
> All the toughness of the cedar,
> All the larch's supple sinews;
> And it floated on the river
> Like a yellow leaf in Autumn,
> Like a yellow water-lily.

Taming a Wild Bear

"Did you ever see a tame bear?" was the stranger's question as he entered our front door.

Having seen my share of tame bears, usually mangy critters in cages, I was trying to think of a way not to see another "tame bear."

"Is it a cub?" I asked.

"No, a full-grown bear."

"Did you catch him as a cub?"

"No, he just came around last spring and I tamed him."

"Someone else must have tamed him first."

"No, he's wild all right."

About that time Mrs. K. came home with her arms full of groceries. I introduced my new aquaintance, Ed Lambert, and she was heartily in favor of going to see the tame bear.

We followed Lambert a few miles out of Aitkin and turned off on a little road disappearing into the woods. Abruptly we found ourselves in a huge and extremely beautiful yard and garden which surrounded a modest but delightful new home. Around the edges, a veritable forest of evergreen trees had been planted and obviously were being carefully pruned.

"Name a tree that will grow in this country and I'll show you one," Lambert said. "For example, here is a nice Douglas fir which is supposed to grow only on the West Coast."

Immediately I became more interested in the Ed Lamberts than I was in any supposedly tame bear.

For an hour we admired the variety of native and exotic trees and lingering fall plants such as the brilliant Japanese lanterns. We could only imagine what the garden, now expertly put to bed for the winter, must have looked like in the midst of summer.

Occasionally, Lambert would walk into the dense forest which surrounded us on all sides and shout, "Here, Beauty. Come, Beauty. Come on out of there, you old son-of-a-gun. What's holding you up?"

He would return, shaking his head and say, "I thought sure he'd be here about now."

Ed's wife invited us in for coffee and we learned about the Lamberts.

Until six years ago they operated a 120-acre farm near the town of Dassel in south central Minnesota. It must have been a well-operated farm because Ed won the coveted Conservation Award.

But, since 1933, Ed had been coming north to this country to fish and hunt, and he always hoped someday to live here. In 1961, he made the break, moved north, bought ten acres of beautiful forest land and carved a large hole in the center of it for his home and spacious lawn and garden.

Asked if he had retired, Lambert said, "No, I just do as I darn please and live up here where I love the wild country and wild things."

Sometimes he works at the nearby grocery store, now and then for the highway department and, being a nurseryman as well as a farmer, he spends a few weeks working at a nursery each year.

The Lamberts interest me because they are typical of middle-aged couples with family responsibilities over who have found pleasure, freedom, work and the good life after fifty. They are tapering off and doing the things they have always wanted to do.

We may see much more of this, and for those who come north for the right reasons it is certainly good. Just wanting to get away from the big city or off the farm is not enough. It is more than running away from something. It is going to find something you really want. And it is figuring out a way to have enough money to be comfortable. Everyone couldn't raise enough produce in his garden to sell it to nearby Shingwauk Resort as Lambert does. But there are many other ways.

In addition to the summer food provided by the garden, Mrs. Lambert has canned and frozen over 200 quarts of fruits and vegetables.

Beauty

Beauty comes to visit

Ed gets his deer every year, and summer or winter there is always fresh fish on hand. During the month of January, the Lamberts fished together in their fish house every day except three. Ed said, "When it gets down to 27 degrees below zero, Ma won't go fishing with me."

Are they happy and content? Apparently completely so. Ed said, "I never had so much fun and I never felt so good."

It was time to leave. Again Ed went to the edge of the forest to shout for Beauty and to scold him for not coming. As we started to drive home, Mrs. Lambert called from the back door, "Beauty's here."

We had to sneak in the back door of the house because anyone coming out the front door is acceptable to Beauty, but he lumbers back into the woods if a stranger approaches from any other direction.

By this time we had heard the story of how Beauty was tamed. He first came last June 26 at 6:50 a.m. when he tore down the bird feeder and ripped the suet basket from the tree.

Ed grabbed his weapon and ran to the front door. But this time his weapon was not his deer rifle but a panful of hot buns which "Ma" had just baked.

She said, "I could have crowned him, running out to the edge of the woods, throwing my fresh buns after that bear as he started running away."

But the buns were an effective weapon for Beauty. He sniffed, turned, came back and had his first taste of Mrs. Lambert's cooking.

A week later he returned and again tore down the bird feeder and suet basket. So a bear-feeding pail and a pan for water were installed. He kept coming back and eating more. His daily ration is now five pounds of dog food, a loaf and a half of bread and miscellaneous sweets such as cake, candy bars and syrup.

One day he came right to the house, stood up, put his paws on the front picture window and peered in.

But now it was time for us to see Beauty. Following Ed, we walked out the front door. Fifty feet away Beauty was emptying his pail of food and finishing off his personal supply of suet. (He doesn't bother the bird feeder any more.)

With a loaf of bread and an additional pan of food, Ed soon had the big, beautiful bear with his glistening black coat and white triangle on his chest standing upright and eating out of his hand. This is certainly not something I would recommend, and I almost swallowed my camera when Mrs. K. walked over and handed him a slice of bread.

Beauty has been following Ed around the garden all summer, but he is still a wild bear and not something to cuddle.

But Ed sure loves his bear. Having eaten his fill, Beauty ambled back into the woods. Ed stood watching him and said, "This is the greatest thing that has ever happened to me. Imagine me, a farmer from Dassel, up in this beautiful country taming a wild bear."

Drab Little Creatures

Hardly anyone likes bats, mice, gophers, moles, shrews or their relatives. Most of us love to have the birds around but dislike, or at best are very indifferent toward, the small mammals. To keep our friends the birds, we provide food, water and shelter and usually forgive them for eating our strawberries and raspberries.

But our main concern with the small animals is how to get rid of them—how to keep the squirrels out of our bird feeders, how to prevent the delightful little white-footed mice from getting into our cabins and homes and how to destroy the moles and gophers that invade our yards.

Do we like the birds better because they fly? That cannot be it because the flying mammals, bats, we hate most of all.

In most respects, the little mammals are much more like us than the birds. But the rabbit, which eats our lettuce, is an enemy while the colorful jay, which pecks our tomatoes, is our friend.

But, in a couple of ways, the senses of man are similar to those of birds and this may make the difference. Like birds, we see color, while to the lesser mammals it is a world of black, white and shades of gray. The fact that man has largely lost his sense of smell also gives him something in common with the birds, which neither smell nor taste.

Biologically, these two similarities between birds and man are quite insignificant. Superficially, they give us some things in common. Being keen-eyed, birds rely on their bright colors and interesting courtship performances during the mating season, and this appeals to us.

Color means nothing to mammals, so they are drab little creatures. The symphony of odors which they can emit and detect, portraying love,

27

Chipmunk

Contemplation

Flight

Success

Robin and young

fear and anger are totally lost to our degenerate olfactory equipment. Who knows, if we could smell a pair of squirrels in courtship it might be more delightful than watching the gaudy display of a peacock.

Also, like us, most of the birds (owls excepted) have poor night vision. They are active in daylight hours when we can watch them while most of the interesting little four-footed animals get all the light their big eyes need from a few twinkling stars. Delightful little flying squirrels may live in our back yards and cavort nightly, sailing from tree to tree without our ever knowing of their presence.

For many months I have been making it increasingly more difficult for the squirrels to get to our bird feeder. They learned to leap to it from the nearest tree, to walk along the top of, or underneath, the thin nylon rope suspending it between two trees. When I put the feeder on top of a steel pipe they learned to climb the pipe. I tried polishing the pipe, greasing it and even icing it. All to no avail.

Recently, one chipmunk, and only one, started climbing the pipe, scrambling across the bottom side of the feeder and up over the edge.

Wasting no time to eat the sunflower seeds on the spot, he fills his cheek pouches to capacity and scurries off to his home at the end of a hole in the ground. On the average, he makes a trip every 90 seconds. He can empty the bird feeder faster than any bird or flock of them.

The smallest animals, such as chickadees and chipmunks, seem to be the most tame. But I don't think they are as much tame as they are fearless. It may also be that man is just too large to be considered a predator by such tiny creatures. Chickadees and chipmunks are probably quite afraid of sparrow hawks and weasels. Large northern pike don't pursue minnows, and wolves don't bother with mice and rabbits if there are deer or moose to be had.

Because we can entice a chipmunk to eat out of our hands doesn't mean he is a particularly friendly animal either. In fact, chipmunks among themselves are quite unsociable. Except for the brief time of mating and when the mother is nursing her young, chipmunks are solitary creatures quite antagonistic to their neighbors.

I don't know why our foxy chipmunk which learned to climb the pole needs to store away so many pounds of sunflower seeds. He is an excellent hibernator and can sleep away the winter.

Not so with tree squirrels. They may stay denned up for a day or two during the severe winter, but they cannot hibernate. To survive they must do two things: get fat in the fall, and store a generous food supply for winter use.

Squirrels rarely store up a large cache in one place, but bury single nuts and acorns in the ground. And, by doing this, they plant a lot of trees. Acorns will usually sprout without being planted, but it has been suggested that almost every hickory tree in America today has been planted by a squirrel.

It is unbelievable that a squirrel remembers the location of the thousands of nuts and acorns he buries, and his sight is of no help when the ground is covered with snow. It can't be luck either because in winter squirrels dig through heavy-crusted snow and find buried nuts with unerring precision. It must be his sensitive nose which tells him where to dig.

In a Michigan study, 251 squirrel caches of acorns were marked. By January 1, ten percent had been dug up and all but two had been recovered by the squirrels by spring.

Mice don't hibernate either, and there are quite a variety of species not to be confused with the detested house mouse which is a European import. But, while we have hundreds of bird clubs, I doubt we will ever have a single mouse club. I even doubt that anyone will put out a mouse feeder this winter.

You Can't Crowd a Wilderness

There is no better mental stimulus than a good argument now and then, and recently I became involved in a dandy. My opponent got it started by expressing violent opposition to removing commercial facilities from the Minnesota wilderness known as the Boundary Waters Canoe Area. When I disagreed, he said, "That makes you a preservationist rather than a conservationist."

Any true conservationist would almost as soon be called a communist as a preservationist, so the argument was off to a fast start. At this point I should interject that I have respect for this gentleman even though our views differ on this point. You just can't have a real fun argument unless you have respect for your opponent.

His view and the view held by many people living adjacent to the canoe area is that it is economically unsound not to exploit this area to the full benefit of local residents. The canoe outfitters seem to be doing all right, but undoubtedly greater financial profits would be derived from this area if it were sprinkled with resorts and all made available by air travel, motorboats or highways. I presume a pop stand on every island would find a certain amount of patronage.

Developed in this way it would no longer be a boundary waters canoe area, but it would admittedly provide recreation for a greater number of people and bring more money into the area.

My aggressive opponent also pointed out that some people are physically unable to paddle a canoe and are thus being unjustly discriminated against by the elimination of more leisurely means of travel. He is firmly convinced that the wilderness aspect of this area must one day be abolished

Bob Carlson and his crow

because, as he said, "We cannot afford to limit a million acres of wilderness to the relatively few who will paddle their way back into it."

There is substance to these arguments, and removal of commercialism from the area is undoubtedly hurting some established businesses and limiting the development of others.

It is always easier to debate in favor of a value that can be expressed behind a dollar sign than it is to prove the intangible worth of aesthetics. Roads, airplanes and motorboats could easily dump another thousand or so people into the area and they would have fun. But they would not experience the never-to-be-forgotten thrill of having lived for a few days or weeks in a wilderness.

Shortly after we were married, my wife and I paddled for four days back into the Boundary Waters Canoe Area. There, with no man-made mark on the landscape and no man-made sound in the air, it was not difficult to imagine that you were the first white man ever to have pulled a canoe up on that particular beach, savored the fragrance of that particular pine forest or cast a plug into the depths of those cool waters. It is an indescribable thrill but one you never forget.

We were never more at peace with the world. But how suddenly it all ended when an airplane dropped down out of the sky, landed directly in front of where we were fishing and two well-dressed businessmen stepped out on the pontoons, made loud vulgar noises and awkwardly cast their lures into the clear waters. They gained a little pleasure, no doubt, but what we had worked so hard for and lost was infinitely greater.

You just can't crowd a wilderness without losing it. So the real point of the argument is—can we afford a wilderness? And is it fair to preclude those who are physically incapable of making the journey and those who are psychologically unfit or simply too lazy to expend the effort necessary to experience wilderness living? I see little honest inequity in the situation and it appears that those who bleed the worst are the ones who have been injured in the pocketbook.

There is no absolute equality. All of us are deprived, in one way or another, of doing things that others can do. The poor man cannot hunt ducks in the best places or fly into Canadian waters for superb trout fishing, but no one feels particularly sorry for him or that he is being discriminated against. Short boys can't make the high school basketball team.

Marsh Marigolds

Small boys are deprived of being members of the football team. Monotones are deprived of the pleasure of making music. All this in no way proves that the hardy souls who are willing to rough it should be denied the opportunity for an inexpensive wilderness vacation just because there are others who cannot.

Can we afford to set aside for them a million acres? If we cannot, ours is indeed a desolate civilization. A million acres of unproductive land is but a mere fraction of the land area we devote to making money. Man does not live by bread alone and certainly the most affluent civilization ever to exist on this earth can afford a little place where hardy men, women and their children may have a glimpse of their rich heritage unspoiled by man.

The U. S. Forest Service has a mandate from at least two presidents and from the Congress to restore and maintain the wilderness nature of the Boundary Waters Canoe Area, and our Canadian neighbors have dedicated an adjoining area of equal size. The U. S. Forest Service is doing its job. They should be commended rather than abused for it. As Forest Supervisor L. P. Neff has said, "There is certainly a place for some wilderness and for this particular kind we have nowhere else to go in the U. S." It will be a sad day when every square foot of the land of this great nation must be dedicated to making the maximum number of dollars.

Compass—Key to Freedom

If he tells you he can travel through the north woods without the use of a compass, you are not listening to a woodsman. You are listening to a fool. No man, Indian or not, has a sense of direction and, as the science of animal behavior progresses, it appears more and more likely that no mammal, fish or fowl has a true sense of direction. Probably even the longest bird migrations are possible because of an instinctive knowledge of stellar navigation rather than any built-in compass.

Except for the migrations, many of which still remain a mystery, animals, including man, learn to travel throughout their environment by memory. By gradually moving out and becoming acquainted with his surroundings, the wild animal establishes his home range. Within this he travels freely but refuses to go beyond its boundaries. Neither man nor fire can push him further. During fox hunts in Nebraska where hundreds of men gather and make a drive over several square miles of land, I have seen jack rabbits come back through the line of men, running almost between their legs rather than be driven outside the range they know.

In the purchase of a simple pocket compass, man can, for a few dollars, buy a better sense of direction than any animal was ever born with. The forester, or anyone trained in the use of the compass, can easily travel ten miles in the day through the wilderness with a certain knowledge that he will not miss his objective by more than a few hundred yards at most.

Hunters usually get no farther than a quarter of a mile off a road, and even this is too far on a cloudy day if they don't have a compass. Of course, people who live in an area get to know it and develop a home range by memory just as any other animal does. But once outside of the range they are just as lost as the city slicker.

One time, while cruising timber for the Lakes States Forest Experiment Station, we met an old Finlander who had spent most of his life in the woods but had no knowledge whatever of the compass. He noticed that we were headed east and said, "Don't go beyond the near edge of the second cedar swamp. No one goes there and you'll never find your way out if you go into it."

He was quite horrified when we told him that we were going not only into that swamp but through it and many miles beyond. He tried hard to dissuade us, and as we left he was sure we would never be seen again.

The old-timer knew every rock and tree within his home range, but he had not learned the magic of the little compass which enables man to travel unerringly throughout the earth.

Of course, buying a compass and dropping it into the pocket of your field jacket falls a bit short of total assurance that you will never get lost. Once, in the woods I heard a hunter shouting for help. I started after him, but he was moving so rapidly that it took some time to get close. Finally I spotted him crashing through the brush at top speed bellowing, "Help!" at every third step. He couldn't hear me call him and I finally had to run him down. He was, of course, frantic with fear, and it took a while to get him calmed down. When I told him he had no business out there without a compass, he said, "Oh, I have a compass." And he took it out to show me.

"What good is a compass?" he asked. "I haven't the slightest idea where I came from or which way is out."

Compasses are of little value without some knowledge of your surroundings. With each compass there should be a map or at least the knowledge of which way to go to a road.

While no one has a built-in sense of direction, developing an awareness of direction produces that comfortable feeling of always knowing where you are. Of course, it also results in a most uncomfortable feeling when you suddenly realize that you don't know which way is north.

Sometimes hunters develop such a strong feeling for direction that they refuse to believe their compasses. But I have yet to hear one of them boast that, as it turned out, he was right and the compass was wrong. As long as the needle on a compass swings freely you can safely assume that one end is pointing approximately north and the other approximately south. This varies a few degrees in different parts of the country and, for some reason which I don't understand, it may change slightly over a period of years. In my youth I was told that a compass points to the north because somewhere up near the North Pole there is a huge magnetic mountain. I never gave it any more thought until I had a son studying physics who explained the magnetic forces surrounding the earth which really control the compass.

With the ever-increasing popularity of recreation in the open spaces, it will be surprising if more people don't learn to use the compass and acquire a feeling for direction. Unfortunately, moss doesn't grow only on the north side of trees so, unaided by a compass, man is virtually chained to the site of habitation. The little pocket compass is the key to his prison cell. With it, a map and the knowledge he can acquire in an hour, the world is his oyster. He can travel anywhere with assurance that he can return at will.

Caught in a Culvert

(Canoeing)

"For something real close to home, that's a nice little canoe trip down Minnehaha Creek into Minneapolis—you've made it, of course."

But I hadn't made it. The next day was bright and warm and my desk became increasingly unbearable as the friend's statement stuck in my mind. It seemed unreasonable that a canoe route should emanate from Gray's Bay, Lake Minnetonka, practically in my back yard, without my having tried it. So, at 2:45 p.m., Mrs. K. and I had deposited a car at the Knollwood Shopping Center and were pushing off into Minnehaha Creek just below Gray's Bay dam. In the center of the canoe sat our neurotic Brittany spaniel. Good wife hadn't favored taking him along, but I explained this was going to be a quiet, uneventful little float down the creek and our nutty dog just might do something which would make a story out of it.

The first mile or two were as peaceful and quiet as I had anticipated, only better. It was surprisingly wild. Muskrats paddled around the new green cattail houses and, in the broad marshy areas surrounding the creek, blackbirds sang as if it were spring. Two hundred crows harassed an owl before darkness would turn the advantage to him. Mallard ducks popped into the air from the margins of the creek. Wood ducks skimmed overhead and countless mudhens, in their cumbersome effort to become airborne, ran and flapped over the water, leaving a silvery wake in the sunlight. Beautiful oak-covered knolls of highland protruded to the creek's edge and you wondered why someone wasn't living there.

Then signs of civilization began to appear. We had expected bridges, but not some fourteen or fifteen of them, including the culverts plus a

About to be "caught in a culvert"

couple of barbed wire fences. But the portages were short and delightful. Where else can you portage a canoe across someone's spacious and beautiful back lawn? Perhaps these home owners enjoy voyageurs in their back yards. Why else would they build bridges with only about a foot clearance under them?

Most exciting of all were rapids, and there were many. We shot the first few with great delight and no mishaps. But they sneak up on you. On calm water you paddle under a bridge only to plunge into a rapids on the other side. Once it didn't go so well. The canoe bow hung up on a rock. This was obviously Mrs. K.'s fault. She should have done something about it.

As any canoeist knows, when the bow of a canoe stops in a rapids, the stern catches up, and soon we were scooting ignominiously down the rapids backwards. This might not have been too bad had I not looked up on the bridge and seen a line of grinning spectators. I had to take time to pull my cap down over my face, and that is when we got hung up again—this time crosswise. There were more spectators. I nonchalantly took out my camera and started taking pictures. What better way to hide one's face?

It suddenly occurred to me that the important thing was to get out of there before someone else showed up with a camera. After all, a picture of outdoor writer Jim Kimball and wife hung up in a canoe in little old Minnehaha Creek might make the front page, and if this story had to be told, I wanted it told my way.

The next bridge was also followed by a sprightly rapids, and good wife insisted we pull over and reconnoiter. I was all for shooting it, but she favored portaging, and when two friendly schoolgirls showed up and agreed with her, I was quickly outvoted. You feel silly portaging a canoe across a highway.

The most dramatic part of our ride sneaked up on us without warning. There was a huge highway fill with two culverts running under it. Proving my contention that highway engineers must hate both people and scenic beauty, the designer of this monstrosity had shrewdly figured out that one culvert would have to be large enough to permit canoes to pass through, but by installing two smaller ones, he could create a real problem for them. One of the culverts was partially clogged with logs and debris and, after our experience, we now hope the other also clogs and the whole road washes out.

By ducking our heads, we found we could start down the other long culvert, and Mrs. K. was having a great time alternately commenting on the great tunnel of love and shouting in order to hear her echo.

But the scheming highway engineer who built the thing was more malevolent than we realized. The culvert slanted downward, which meant the water got higher and the clearance above it less. We had to lie flat on our backs in the bottom of the canoe. But even this didn't work. The two ends of the canoe caught on the top of the culvert and we stopped. At this point the nutty dog between us contracted a severe case of claustrophobia and started walking on my face.

I considered the case of letting air out of tires when a truck got stuck under a bridge, and it seemed that tipping the canoe to get it half full of water might accomplish the same result. But, as we were lying on our backs in it, this would certainly be the last resort. By reaching up and pushing on the culvert, the canoe moved gradually forward. Bumping and bouncing along the corrugated ceiling, at last we were out. Canoeists should erect a statue of a sneering highway engineer at this point to throw rocks at.

From here on the shoreline became increasingly more developed. We paddled through spacious back yards and viewed lovely homes. It seemed we had covered a span in history rather than a few geographical miles as the muskrat houses gave way to side-by-side people houses.

This is really an interesting little canoe trip, but not necessarily inexpensive—not when you end up in a shopping center with a wife who is not only hungry, but is carrying along her charge-a-plate.

Camp Courage

It was not an enjoyable experience, but it did something for me. In addition to writing about wildlife and natural resources, it has been my happy lot to work with and write about people who are strong and rugged; the robust and self-sufficient; men and women of strength and stamina.

No one could be more psychologically ill-equipped than I to spend a day with a hundred crippled children at Camp Courage. The body of a normal child is a glorious thing—agile, quick, sensitive, and responsive; bursting with energy and quick to recover from fatigue and bruises. It was meant to run, skip, climb, fall and jump up, to chase and be chased and to express those intricate inward emotions of youth.

To see a hundred little human bodies devoid of these gifts we take so for granted is a sobering experience. They are victims of cerebral palsy, muscular dystrophy, blindness and many other diseases. The first-time observer must force himself to understand that within these expressionless bodies are to be found minds, souls, emotions, needs and dreams which are often quite normal.

I rode with them on a trailer behind a jeep. It was nothing. A normal kid would have passed us on the run. I walked with them, some in wheel chairs, some led and some almost carried, a few hundred feet into the woods. It, too, was nothing. A healthy boy could have traveled farther and faster doing somersaults.

But it really was something. This is what I had to force myself to realize. To these cheated kids it was ecstatic. Jogging over a road in a trailer or poking across a lake in a pontoon boat is an exciting experience —when you thought you never would or never could.

44

The miracle of nature touches them all.

The love of nature and all her elegance is not confined only within robust bodies. These kids squealed with delight and chattered excitedly as the trailed bumped, and they complained when it stopped.

As the counselor, affectionately known as "Nature Jim," took the hand of a girl and ran her sensitive fingers down the rough bark of a tree until it felt the soft moss near the base, her sightless blue eyes widened in amazement.

They nibbled bits of the nutty flavored Solomon's-seal root which Jim dug, and they poked trembling fingers into moist rotting wood while being told how soil was built. All watched when a spastic hand was held steady while a little white worm was dropped in its palm. Were the squeals expressions of fear, excitement, or delight?

I didn't know. There were many things I didn't understand. Why were those fine, healthy college girls, employed as counselors, holding crippled bodies, pushing wheel chairs, pressing leaves into crippled hands and talking sign language? What good could it do? What use? What possible benefit?

I couldn't understand. I wanted to leave. I could hardly resist the impelling urge to swing my healthy legs in their longest stride until I was far back into the vigorous, virile forest—forever out of sight and sound of the infirm, insecure and helpless. But there had to be answers, so I struggled not to run—physically or mentally.

Camp Courage itself is a thing of great beauty, as it certainly should be. It is located on Cedar Lake between the towns of Annandale and Maple Lake. From the large, handlike hardwood forest behind the camp, fingers of woods extend over the rolling terrain through beautiful lawns, gardens and redwood buildings to the beach.

Each building has character and charm. Expansive windows, beautiful views and vaulted, beamed ceilings imparted a spacious sense of simple freedom—a feeling of uncluttered, unconfined room for expanding thoughts and dreams, if not actions. You wonder if the architect, the late Larry Hovick, worked from a vision. You know he understood the needs of active minds in crippled bodies.

Returning home with Bill Shoenbohm, executive director of the Minnesota Society for Crippled Children and Adults, and Paul Scudder, director of Camp Courage, I learned many things about the camp.

Ten years ago 70% of the kids were polio victims. Thanks to medical research, this has fallen to 17%. Now the largest number are afflicted with cerebral palsy.

One major problem is parental overprotectionism. Mothers of the many children who would benefit greatly from camp say, "I can't stand the thought of my child being without me for two weeks."

The list of organizations and individuals who have donated time and money to Camp Courage is long and makes you realize that people do care. Rabbits, ducks, raccoons, foxes, spotted fawns and other wildlife can be seen and touched in the little zoo. The donated Fragrance Garden is a delight to children who can only touch and smell, as well as to those who can see.

Two nurses and a doctor are always on hand. From a complete weather station the children make weather predictions twice daily. During his twelve days at camp, each child goes on five or six "cook-outs" and camps out overnight twice. The effort involved in one of these "camp-outs" is staggering, and you understand why there is one counselor or program worker for every three children.

The capacity of Camp Courage is 96. Current expansion will increase it to 166 next year. This will substantially increase the 600 annual capacity.

But statistics didn't answer the basic question which so disturbed my ill-adjusted mind. What do you accomplish? How do you stand it? What is the objective?

There had been a glimmer of understanding when blind Pamela groped for her nature guide's hand and said, "Thank you, Jim, I liked it."

The glimmer of light grew as Paul Scudder and Bill Schoenbohm talked. "We want to give these kids the ordinary experiences that we take for granted and they have been deprived of—those rewarding out-of-doors experiences." ". . . give them a broader outlook on life." "The new speech and hearing unit will be more therapeutic than recreational." "Both the kids and adults are *fun* to work with." "You have to remember that these kids are basically healthy but have limitations." "Our young college counselors are in it for what they can *give,* not for what they get out of it." "These crippled kids face tremendous challenges, and these challenges become your challenges."

I began to understand why so many give so much to Camp Courage. It became clearer when I read what a young counselor had written: "The first night in the cabin, I was overcome—everything was physical—crutches, braces, catheters . . . things I had never been in contact with before in my life. That, however, was the extent of any preoccupation with the physical. As I continued working with the kids, I realized how little a body means. They were homesick, selfish, happy, or generous, and the working abilities of their bodies had nothing to do with it. I reached the point where I never again noticed or regarded them as "handicapped," and that continued throughout the summer."

Conservation in the Curriculum

Recently our son returned from the University of Chicago to spend a little time in the peace and quiet of a small town and a lake cabin to write his Ph.D. thesis in physics.

I have always stood in awe of, and felt quite inferior to, the mathematicians, physicists and other scientists whose great discoveries have so altered and improved man's way of life. I mentioned this to my son and was surprised to hear him reply, "Yes, but probably the greatest problem now facing our civilization is the destruction and pollution of our environment."

When a son tells the old man that his field of endeavor, conservation, is the important one, it does a great deal for the old boy's ego. And this set me to pondering the great issues of modern man. Perhaps my thoughts will stimulate you to better ones.

First, there are the little conservation projects—birdfeeders, birdhouses, gardens, fish-rearing ponds, bits of pheasant habitat, improving a trout stream, raising and releasing pheasants or ducks and developing a corner of a farm for wildlife.

These little do-it-yourself conservation projects may not influence the destiny of man, but they produce tangible results which we can see, touch, enjoy and take pride in. Combined, they form the conservation primer which develops interest and appreciation of our earth. Their importance lies not in what they achieve in conservation but in altering the attitude of the doer. But they can be classified as little more than selfish entertainment if they do not stimulate us to seek out the bigger issues.

We live in a world that is rapidly becoming crowded and dirty, a world that is having its checks and balances, which have been developing for millions of years, thrown out of kilter. Our earth is being littered, bulldozed and paved, our waters polluted and our air fouled. Man has become so adept at regulating the plants and animals living on earth that the ecology of our planet is being disrupted.

Do we have the will and are we willing to make the sacrifice to do something about it? Only if we believe in something bigger than ourselves, or at least beyond our generation, because the price will be high and the sacrifice great.

I am not so concerned about this generation. The earth, though further abused, will hold together as long as we adults will need it. But what of the next generation, and the next? What will our legacy be to them? Our greatest obligation is to teach our children to love and guard the earth.

Looking into the delicate structure of a moccasin flower or peering upward through the branches of a giant oak, we stand in awe. We don't understand, but we marvel at it. But what does the city-raised child stand in awe of?

He sees giant buildings and knows his generation will build them bigger and better. He knows that the cars of his generation will be more streamlined and faster. Everything around him is made by man and can be made better by men of the future.

All he sees is within his comprehension. There is nothing to marvel at, nothing to stand in awe of, nothing that is sacred, nothing to make him humble. The natural environment which supports his life is remote, and he thinks it can surely be improved by the technology of man.

We should not forget the words of historian H. G. Wells who wrote, "The history of man is the story of a hungry animal in search of food." The world's greatest population centers were once in the fertile valleys of the Nile and the Euphrates. Overuse of these lush environments destroyed them, converted them into eroded deserts; and man, the hungry animal, moved elsewhere in search of food.

But now every fertile corner of the earth is becoming crowded and predictions of the unbelievable numbers of people to be occupying this earth in a relatively few years must frighten us all, and the moon promises to be a poor substitute for earth. The hungry animal's search has ended, but his numbers continue to increase.

As individuals and as organizations, the greatest conservation power of our generation lies in our right to vote and even more in our ability to influence votes. Our democracy may have faults, but it is a democracy that works. The people do rule. They get what they want. It is the obligation of people living in a democracy to be informed if they are to vote and to be better informed if they are to influence votes. The power of an intelligent letter written to a legislator or a congressman is more potent than most of us would believe.

Conservationwise, there is only one thing we can do which is more important than influencing the laws of our nation. This is influencing the minds of our children. We have been the most destructive generation the earth has had to put up with. The generation to come will have infinitely greater powers than we have, and if their attitude toward their environment is not better than ours their destructive force may be comparable to that of the Ice Age.

So, our greatest obligation as conservationists is to teach our children to understand, appreciate and love their natural environment. This should be done in schools, but it is making pitifully slow progress there. The few school administrators who are attempting to do the job should be given every possible encouragement and support. Unfortunately, there are not many of them.

At various times, and in three different states, I have attempted to get conservation taught in schools. Each effort met with total failure. Each time I got the standard pat answers. "Our curriculum is already full. In order to teach conservation, what do you want us to leave out? English? Mathematics? History? Science? Reading and writing?"

I didn't have the answer then, but I have excellent answers now. Two of them. First, you don't have to leave any course out. Knowledgeable teachers with a deep interest in conservation assure me that conservation can be taught in conjunction with all of these courses, and it would improve them.

The second answer is, if you can't combine conservation with other subjects, leave out any subject you like, because conservation is the most important one. Is it more important that our children learn to master cube root and quote a few lines of Chaucer or that they learn to protect the environment which determines not only their standard of living but the strength of this nation and the destiny of man?

Our earth has remarkable power to heal its wounds. It has withstood everything from molten lava to the crushing devastation of great ice sheets. I have no fear that in the long run the earth will survive the destructive powers of man. It is the survival of man and not the survival of earth which is in question. We may destroy the environment which sustains our lives, but in a mere million years or so the order and the ecology of the planet will be reestablished. Only man will be missing.

The spring peepers and swamp tree frogs sing in early spring.

Summer Morn

We are living at the lake most of the time this summer. But there are the frequent mad rushes to the big city to take care of those details involved in making a living.

After three hectic and horribly hot days in Minneapolis, I drove back to the cabin. As I enjoyed my evening snack before bed, a voice on the radio announced an 81-degree temperature in the Twin Cities. The mercury in our porch thermometer stood at 63. I crawled into bed, pulled a blanket over me and slept so soundly that it seemed like only an instant later I was awake, refreshed and seeing early dawn.

The red-eyed vireos were just beginning their robinlike songs, repeated at one-second intervals. Under the burdensome chores of raising a hungry family, most songbirds find little to sing about in midsummer. But not so with red-eyed vireos.

The morning and evening songs from a marsh always intrigue and mystify me. Though most frogs have ceased their spring clatter, two species continued to call, and I'm not really sure which they are. I think one is the mink frog which has a slightly metallic quality to his voice and has been said to "resemble closely the sound produced by striking a long nail on the head with a hammer and driving it into a heavy timber." And these frogs continue to breed and sing well into August.

The other sound was deep and rough and I would guess it to be a bullfrog except that we have no bullfrogs here. I used to think that this noise was made by big snapping turtles, but Dr. Walter Breckenridge, director of the University of Minnesota Museum of Natural History, says that to the best of his knowledge no turtles give voice and that the well-known quotation, "and the voice of the turtle is heard in our land," was spoken of the turtle dove. And Breckenridge is no doubt right. He is not only the best naturalist I know, but he has authored the book "Reptiles and Amphibians of Minnesota."

I have often wondered why so many people diligently study and learn the songs of birds and remain blissfully ignorant of the variety of amphibian songs that emanate from a marsh.

When the mind starts asking questions and pondering imponderables, it is not going back to sleep again, so I got up to enjoy the dawn. I wasn't really hungry, but I ate half a can of pears so I could have my first pipe of the day without violating my rule never to smoke before breakfast.

As I left the cabin, Joe, our nutty Brittany spaniel, bounded out from under the porch to greet and escort me on a morning walk. But this was a very still, foggy, dewy morning when one feels almost obliged to tiptoe along the trails—a sensitive, fragile morning which could be shattered by a silly dog racing around and pointing at everything from frogs to chipmunks. I didn't feel inclined to argue the point with Joe, so I just stood around until he crawled back under the porch for another hour of sleep.

It was the kind of foggy morning that mallard ducks seem most to enjoy, perhaps because their voices sound so loud. From both sides of the point and out on the island the hen mallards talked back and forth. One made a short flight and lit almost in front of where I stood on the dock. And another, with four half-grown young, swam out of the fog. On the still water they looked as big as a battleship with four accompanying cruisers. I've always wondered why ducks look so big in a fog. Perhaps it's because they get close before you see them and they are really much nearer than they seem.

Mallard drakes have gone—left our lake to gather someplace with the rest of "the boys" in a secluded spot where they molt and become flightless until their worn wing feathers have been replaced with new. Later the hens will molt, too, but not until their responsibilities to their young have been fulfilled.

I don't understand the midsummer activity of hen mallards. They perform strange antics and sometimes quack so incessantly that you are sure they aren't ducks at all but one small boy playing with his father's

Fog-saturated spider webs glisten in morning light.

duck call. Perhaps they are bragging to each other about the fine broods of young they are raising. I can't read their minds, but they appear quite happy.

Morning did not come with a sudden burst as it does in mid-June, and I realized that the longest days have passed and that, though the seasons lag, fall could not be far away.

This must have been a good summer for catbirds. They seem to be everywhere, not singing their melodious song which so resembles the brown thrasher or the mockingbird, but, apparently guarding the nest and young, they uttered the midsummer "meow" which would fool even a cat.

The pontoon boat, its chairs, table, rails and canopy were all laced together in shining gauze—hundreds of spider webs, which, saturated with the fog, glistened in the morning light. For a moment I wondered how so many spiders could have suddenly gotten onto a boat anchored between four posts with no bridge to land. Then I realized that these were the airborne spiders which, shortly after hatching, climb aloft, construct a parachute of gauze, swing free and trust the summer winds to carry them to a new home.

From rafts of floating round leaves, buds of water lilies reaching a few inches above the surface were opening into big yellow flowers. Goldenrod was starting to bloom and the big cone-shaped flower clusters of the sumac were pinkish red on the exposed side and more green where shaded.

But even the sumac leaves, the first to change color in the fall, showed no sign of red. It was still midsummer and the land was lush and green. Jewelweed was in full bloom and it would be some time before its sensitive seed pods would explode at the touch, dispensing its seeds for several feet.

As I started back to the cabin, the snowshoe hare that has been tantalizing our dog all summer, hopped clumsily down the road ahead. His instinctive fear of dogs, if he ever had any, was being allayed by this silly dog that points but never bites. He may even have taken pride in being the most pointed-at rabbit in the community.

Hiking back to the cabin to my breakfast of bacon, eggs, toast and hot coffee, I decided that the best thing about 24-hour days is that they are divided into four parts as distinct as the four seasons: morning, midday, evening, and night. I don't know which is the best, but morning is the least familiar to most of us.

Showering Leaves

Rolling reluctantly out of bed at 6 a.m. one fall Sunday, shuffling out of the north woods cabin door into the cold, still morning air and scurrying down the "path," the sole objective in my sleep-fogged mind was returning to a warm bed before full consciousness brought further sensitivity to the cold.

But the objective was lost. Half-closed eyes opened wide in the brilliant rays of a sun in the east rising to the first blue sky to be seen in weeks. The sun shown from below the horizon, too, in a glistening path of brilliance across placid water. I was awake.

It was cold, but standing still, body heat seemed not to dissipate into the motionless air. Fall had come to the north country. Warm autumn colors had descended like a blanket over the cool greens of the forest as if to protect it from the chill of night. With shortened days and slanting rays, Sun was once more losing its annual fall war with North Wind for dominion.

It would be spring before Sun could again win the ceaseless and eternal struggle, but this morning it was winning a battle. Walking to the dock, an eggshell crust on the soft soil crushed under foot. It had been a cold night. The rickety little dock was coated with white frost, and paper-thin ice along the shore flashed its miracle of design in the sunlight. Rushes, protected by the summer warmth begrudgingly given up by the water below, were still lush and green. A threesome of mallards stretched strong wings over the water and, with a thrust of power, burst into the air. Feeble asthmatic utterances of the drake, followed by a resonant quacking of one of the hens, shattered the morning stillness.

Far to the north, geese were calling, and somewhere in the fog rising from the lake a pair of loons shouted across the still water. Suddenly they burst from the fog in full flight and, laughing as they flew, passed directly overhead. The white bellies of their dirigible-shaped bodies, pointed and black-tipped on both ends, glistened in the rising sun and the slow beat of their powerful wings made a swishing sound unlike that of any duck.

It was quiet again as the sun edged a little higher on the low rainbow-like arc it would make across the southern sky. The raucous calls of a pair of blue jays startled me into reality and I ambled back along the woods road.

Leaves of sumac, usually the first to predict summer's end in warning red, were still green but shriveled into sudden death by the early freeze. Musing at their apparent shame in being caught unaware of the changing seasons, I heard strange crackling sounds in the forest. Puzzled for a time, it resembled a thousand mice jumping about in dry leaves—or was it hail falling from a blue sky?

Looking above the forlorn sumac, I saw the most amazing shower of leaves descending into the still morning air. Ash trees, always first to shed summer foliage, had been smitten in the night. As the sun shown first on the treetops and slowly sent its rays down into the foliage as it rose, the lifeless leaves, held now only by crystals of ice, embarked on their descent to become mold and nourishment on the forest floor. It seemed strange that leaves which had held firm against the unfriendly elements so long should now, after the freeze, be brought to earth not by wind, rain or hail, but by their friend, the sun.

A ruffed grouse, lingering near the drumming log which is home base for him throughout the year, burst from a thicket with a roar of beating wings. His erratic flight through the forest brought the first movement of air since the freeze. In his wake the shower of falling leaves gave the amusing impression of a bird flying right out of his feathers.

A gentle breeze drifted listlessly in from the lake. Seemingly amazed and delighted that leaves which had resisted its big brother winds all summer now snapped and sailed through the air, it reveled in the sport until the air was filled with floating and fluttering flakes of brown and gold.

Soon the ash trees stood bare. Rid of their vulnerable leaves, trunk and twigs were ready for the onslaught of winter. But, divest of green

Ruffed grouse drumming

chlorophyll which combines sunlight and water to produce food for mother tree, leaves of oak, maple, aspen, basswood and birch showed their true colors of scarlet orange and yellow. Their work forever done, they linger aloft to enjoy their golden age and to enrich the scene by the beauty of their being.

Why Do They Sing?

(Bird Songs)

To make beautiful music, birds, like poets, should be hungry or have a lost love. At least birds seem to do their best singing before breakfast, and it is known that bachelor birds sing more ardently than those with mates.

We like to think that birds sing for the sheer joy of being alive in the beautiful spring, and all that. This could be part of it, but they appear to use their songs to advertise for a mate, defend their territory, drive away enemies, convey information about approaching danger and probably much more.

To most of us, a song sparrow always sounds the same, but it has been learned that one song sparrow may have twenty variations to his call.

For the most part, singing is left to the males; but female cardinals, rose-breasted grosbeaks and some others also sing. In fact, some pairs of tropical birds sing a duo.

In one experiment, a number of birds were made deaf and kept in captivity. They continued to sing, mate and behave normally. All went well until they started raising the young, which all starved to death because their calls for food could not be heard by the parents.

It has been proved that birds do "talk" to each other, but not with intention as humans do. Their talk and the response to it always seems to be instinctive. Therefore, they probably never learned to lie to each other.

Baby pheasants or prairie chickens which have just hatched and had no time to learn anything will hide and "freeze" at their mother's warning call and come when she clucks.

I knew a priest named Father Tibisar who raised all sorts of birds as a hobby in Rollingstone, Minnesota. He said that baby pheasants or quail raised under a setting hen would run off and leave their foster mother immediately after hatching because they did not instinctively recognize her call. However, if he kept them penned up with her for a few days they would learn her calls and respond to them.

It was long wondered whether birds sang their songs instinctively or whether their songs were learned. Several experiments have been conducted by hatching and raising birds where they could not hear the calls of any other birds. It was discovered that the songs of some birds are almost entirely innate. They instinctively learned to sing. Other species did not develop songs anything like those of their parents. In one experiment, artificially incubated blackbirds were exposed to the songs of various songbirds and learned to sing like them.

Birds of the same species may have calls which vary in different parts of their range. The French crow, for example, did not respond to the warning call of an American crow.

Frequently birds have warning calls which are recognized by other species as well as birds of their own kind. They also have calls which indicate different kinds of danger. Just as Paul Revere had signals, "one if by land and two if by sea," the domestic rooster says "gogogogock" if a dog or man approaches on the ground, but when a hawk flies over, he says "raaaaay." (My chicken English may not be perfect.) Strangely enough, many small birds use essentially the same two types of calls to give a warning of danger—a clucking or chirping to indicate ground danger, and drawn-out notes to warn of aerial attack.

Of course, birds sing most in the spring during the courtship and mating season. Singing wanes with the duties of raising a family, but may start again in the fall.

If you get up, or are still up, a half hour before sunrise on a spring morning, you will notice that some species of birds start to sing ahead of others. Cardinals and song sparrows start early, while house wrens wait for two hundred times more light. Most of them start between thirty and fifteen minutes before sunrise, depending on whether it is clear or cloudy. A bright moon may get them started a little ahead of schedule. In the far north where summer nights are short, snow buntings get only two or three hours sleep. I wonder if birds ever take "cat naps."

Birds sing most in the early morning and frequently have a short songfest just before bed. A few keep it up all day. Some patient soul kept tabs on a red-eyed vireo for a full day and learned that he sang 22,197 times.

In a small northern Minnesota town I once stopped at a beer tavern (to get change for a parking meter) and heard a young Finn expertly imitating a variety of songbirds. He could describe each bird and its habits, but to my amazement, he didn't know the name of a single one. In fact, when I told him their names, the young man showed little interest. These woodland birds were his friends. He knew them well—so what's in a name?

The art of identifying birds by sound rather than sight is not easy, but most gratifying once you have achieved a measure of success. When you can lie under a tree in the forest and identify twenty invisible birds, you have become a successful bird listener. As a lazy man's sport, bird listening beats bird watching except for one thing. There is always one bird song you can't identify, so you are forced to leave your comfortable bed under the tree, take up your binoculars and pursue the stranger.

The Chiselers

(Woodpeckers)

When April arrives most of us quit buying sunflower seeds and erect birdhouses in order to keep our winged entertainers in the yard where we can enjoy them. Where natural tree cavities are scarce, houses do increase bird numbers. In a Maryland chestnut orchard the addition of 98 birdhouses resulted in a 300% to 400% increase in the number of birds.

There is one group of birds which I particularly admire, not because they usually scorn our rent-free housing projects, but because they are interesting in many ways. These are the woodpeckers.

Most of them are quite capable of chiseling out their own homes in anything from a dead tree to a healthy oak, and they don't always overlook fence posts and telephone poles. It is said that Mr. Woodpecker goes around tapping on trees and things until he strikes a sound which appeals to his mate, which flies over and gently taps with him. This is the signal to start home building and the chips begin to fly. The entrance hole is aimed up to keep out the rain. Then the chiselers, taking turns at about five-minute intervals, work down to the desired depth. The white eggs are laid on the chips at the bottom of the hole.

Digging these holes is no haphazard business. Like a woodsman with an ax, their sharp bills are driven first on one side and then the other until large chips are torn out. Their bills are not only sharp, but backed up by heavy skulls which act as a hammer driving a chisel. This is only part of their specialized equipment.

Most woodpeckers have two toes in front and two behind which give them a fine pair of clamps for driving their sharp claws into the

63

Hooded merganser less than an hour old. Hatched in a tree cavity made by a pileated woodpecker.

bark. They don't come down trees head first as nuthatches do, because they rely on their exceptionally stout spikelike tails for props.

Like all birds, woodpeckers have exceptionally good hearing, and it is believed they locate, with their ears, beetles, worms and ants boring beneath the bark and far into the heart of trees. They may also detect insect tunnels or hollow spots by tapping on the tree and listening for a difference in sound just as you tap on the wall in an effort to locate one of the 2 × 4 studs when you want to hang a picture.

Redheaded woodpeckers have always been a favorite of mine, perhaps because they were plentiful around the farm when I was a boy. It seems to me that these beautiful birds became quite rare, but have increased somewhat in recent years. They are frequently killed on highways and, like flickers, other woodpeckers and bluebirds, they are driven out of their homes by starlings.

One of the most interesting things about woodpeckers is their tongues. When I was a small boy my older brother tossed me a dead flicker and said, "Pull out its tongue." I shall never forget the tremendously long, barbed tongue which I pulled out of its beak.

Flickers are a brand of woodpecker which stays pretty close to the ground and lives largely on ants. When you see them in the yard poking their bills into the ground, they are probably cleaning out an anthill for you. All woodpeckers have these long tongues for insect probing. The tongue can be so long because it is attached far back. The flicker's tongue starts at the tip of his upper bill and circles clear around the back of his skull and out his beak in front.

The redheaded woodpecker and some others store a winter's supply of acorns in holes they have cut into trees. During the winter they will defend this hoarded food supply by attacking woodpeckers or even blue jays which might move in for a free meal.

Sometimes the redheads aren't too smart about this storage problem, however. In one instance, several hundred acorns were poked through a knothole into an empty cabin. Another case, even more ridiculous, was that of the redheaded woodpecker poking acorns into a hole in a telephone pole. The only trouble with this was that the hole went clear through the pole and the acorns kept dropping out the other side.

In general, woodpeckers are the forester's best friend, taking a heavy toll of destructive forest insects. One exception is the sapsucker which makes those funny rows of oval-shaped holes which not only provide sap for him to drink, but attract insects which he eats. Sometimes the sap ferments and the indulging sapsucker goes around flying into trees or becomes too drunk to fly at all.

Woodpeckers don't win many honors as vocalists, but as drummers they have no peers. They drum love songs to their mates and threats to other birds invading their territory. They love to drum on hollow trees which put out a fine resonant sound. They also have fun on houses with loose boards or on tin roofs. If you have one playing a tune on your roof each morning about sunrise, you probably don't like woodpeckers as well as I do.

Building a Birdhouse

Like you, I, too, have always wanted to be famous for something. At long last, I am about to mount the pinnacle of success because of a startling new architectural design. Of course, some of the ideas have been "lifted" from various existing plans, but who worries about the meager sin of plagiarism when he stands trembling with anticipation on the brink of fame and glory.

I have designed a birdhouse that *anyone* can build. You may be skeptical that there is a plan so simple that anyone can follow it. Many a dad has put his hand on his boy's shoulder and said, "Come, son, I'll teach you how to build a birdhouse." Hours later, Dad had a pile of split boards, a bruised thumb and all Junior had been taught were a few words that do not appear in the dictionary.

But as will be later revealed, my plan has been put to the supreme test.

Of course, you will need lumber, and there is more than one way to get it. If a new house is being built in your block, there will be many scraps lying around. You might, on a dark night, go quietly to your back door . . . but you'd better just let out the cat, go to bed and the next morning go over and beg a few short scraps of 1 × 4 and 1 × 6 boards. You will find the builder remarkably generous with scraps—if they are less than a foot long.

If you prefer buying to begging, go to the lumber yard, buy two boards, each two feet long. One is called a 1 × 4 and the other a 1 × 6. When you discover the 1-inch boards are only ¾″ thick and that they are nearly a half inch short of being four inches and six inches wide, don't call your lumberman a cheat. Lumbermen have been getting by with this for so many generations that they consider it perfectly honest. Besides, if you do not have a brace and a one-inch bit at home, you want to cajole your friendly lumberman into drilling a one-inch hole in the center of your four-inch board, two inches from the end. Then you can cheer him up by buying a dime's worth of 5-penny nails. They love these big sales.

Now, assuming that you or someone has drilled the one-inch hole, the only tools you need are a saw, a square and a hammer. Starting with the end of the four-inch board which has the hole in it, cut off a $6\frac{1}{2}''$ piece, then a $4\frac{1}{8}''$ piece. Mark them "front," "bottom," and the remaining one, "back." From the six-inch board, cut three pieces, all $6\frac{1}{2}''$ long for sides and top.

Drill a couple of drain holes about a quarter of an inch in size in the small bottom piece. If you don't have a drill, hold a big nail over the stove with a pair of pliers and have fun burning holes. Next, keeping everything even at the top, nail the two sides on the back, nail in the bottom and nail on the top.

With a rasp, plane or paring knife, round off the outside top edge of the front. Nail it in with one nail on each side, two inches down from the top of the roof. This permits the bottom of the front to swing out so the house can be cleaned out. Another nail driven part way in on one side will hold the front in place and your birdhouse is done.

Should your critics chide you about a few bent nails or bad joints, tell them that birds prefer rustic dwellings.

What you have built is a wren house and it should be placed between five and eight feet from the ground. If you are close to an open field, you might try one for bluebirds by making the hole $1\frac{1}{2}''$ in diameter, and it wouldn't hurt to make the house a couple of inches higher. Put it on a fence post or something not over five feet from the ground. With the $1\frac{1}{2}''$ hole you might even attract a tree swallow, chickadee, downy woodpecker or perhaps an English sparrow.

If you are going to put birdhouses out this year, don't wait. It is already plenty late. House wrens do not start arriving until the middle of April or the first of May, but bluebirds often arrive before the middle of March. In many species, the males come first to scout out the territory, so it is good to have the house up well in advance of nest-building time.

Mrs. K.'s birdhouse

The eager male house wren even starts building the nest before his mate arrives.

But can you actually build your own birdhouse? Yes. I put the plan to the supreme test by laying this column, the boards and tools on the workbench, leading my wife to the scene and going upstairs.

It should be explained at this point that while at various points in her career Mrs. K. has achieved some success with tennis racquets, ball bats, canoe paddles, knitting needles, bread pans and paintbrushes, she doesn't know in which hand to hold a hammer or saw.

From the basement came sounds of sawing and pounding, inter-
mingled with exclamations and giggles and climaxed, in thirty minutes,
with an exuberant shout of "Eureka!"

The end product is a woodworker's nightmare, but she dares me to
put my neat power saw model up beside hers and let the wrens be the
judges—a dare I don't intend to take.

Young Robin

Why the Robin Cocks His Head

(Bird Eyes)

It is amazing how much you learn about bird behavior just by finding out how their eyes work. Somehow I got interested in birds' eyes and began reading about them.

Now I know why a robin cocks his head when he is hunting worms, why a chicken pokes his head back and forth while walking and why a mudhen does the same thing when he swims. There is a good reason why a bittern standing in a swamp pokes his head straight up in the air when he is disturbed, and it isn't the reason I thought it was.

Bird eyes may not look very large, but actually they are enormous, taking up more head space than the bird's brain. Apparently flying demands a large picture screen with every detail sharp. A sparrow hawk's vision is eight times as good as man's. The visual acuity of birds is not matched by any other living creature. Large hawk and eagle eyes are as big as man's, and ostriches have eyeballs nearly as large as tennis balls.

Most birds seem to possess better focusing devices than we have, too. Instantly they can shift their focus from a distant object to a tiny insect an inch from their beaks. So it seems they have built-in magnifying glasses as well as built-in telescopes. It is hard to believe that when you are looking at a bird through a pair of six or seven-power binoculars he can still see you better than you see him.

Of course, bird eyes vary a great deal between species in accordance with their way of life. I once kept a great horned owl for a couple of months while his broken wing was healing. Every time I tossed him a rabbit to eat, he would back off and look at it for awhile before pouncing

71

Robin feeding young

on it. I thought he was probably afraid of it, but that wasn't really the case. Owls are farsighted and he had to back up to see what it was.

Hawks, usually looking down for prey, see best out of the lower part of their eyes. When they want to look at the sky they sometimes turn their heads upside down to see it better.

Birds have a third eyelid called the nictitans. This transparent membrane is an ingenious device for cleansing and moistening their eyes without closing them. Loons and diving ducks have a very specialized nictitans. In its center is a clear lens-shaped window with a high refractive index that acts like a contact lens when the bird is under water. This nictitans is not only brushlike on the inner surface for cleansing the eye with tears, but has a fold on the margin which acts as a windshield wiper on the return trip.

Birds, like men, have cones and rods on the retina of their eyes. The cones detect color and the rods are more sensitive to light. The cones are grouped in the central focusing spot or fovea for color detection. Birds which are active in daylight have more of these cones and can detect color better than owls which must see at night. It seems incredible that owls can see with about one-hundredth the amount of light that man requires.

The position of a bird's eyes in his head is directly related to his way of life. Songbirds which are constantly in danger of being attacked have their eyes on the sides of their heads and can see in all directions at once. I had always been told that robins hunting worms in the yard cocked their heads in order to hear the worms—though I could never quite imagine a soft, slimy worm in moist grass setting up much of a clatter. The fact is, his eyes are not very movable so he turns his head in order to bring one eye into sharp forcus where he suspects there may be a worm.

I always thought that bitterns, also known as "shite-pokes," "slough pumps," or "thunder pumps," when disturbed in a swamp poked their heads straight up in the air to imitate a stick and thus avoid detection. But that isn't it at all. Being frog and lizard catchers, their eyes point down to better see their prey. The only way they can look ahead is to stick their bills straight up in the air so their eyes look forward.

The eyes of an owl look straight ahead much as ours do. Like most small boys, I was told that if you walked around one enough times, he would wring his own neck trying to watch you. I could never make it work. Owls can't turn their eyes much, so to compensate for this, they have developed a very flexible neck and can turn their heads more than 270 degrees.

Of course, a woodcock has about the silliest eyes of them all. They are so high on his head that they look up better than down when he is feeding. Actually, the vision from his two eyes overlaps more behind than in front. Perhaps he is more interested in where he has been than where he is going.

There seems to be some question as to whether or not birds, even when looking at an object with both eyes at once, have true binocular vision. When we look at something with both eyes open we see it in stereoptic, that is, in three dimensions and we can determine the distance quite well. Some automatic computer or range finder in our heads seems to take care of this. This may, or may not, be the case with birds. But even birds that look at things with only one eye at a time have a technique for obtaining depth perception. Many shore birds, such as sandpipers, bob their heads up and down, thus getting two views of an object with one eye instead of using both eyes at once. Other birds, such as coots swimming in the water, bob their heads back and forth in order to obtain the effect of binocular vision.

However, this does not appear to be the only reason for head bobbing. A walking chicken moves his head back the exact distance of his stride forward. Thus his bobbing head is actually stationary most of the time. This makes it much easier for him to detect the movement of any object which might be either a source of food or danger.

I wouldn't really recommend this head-bobbing procedure to improve your vision. It's strictly for the birds.

Squirrel rocking bird feeder, eating peanut butter.

Learning To Be a Birder

Last week's bundle of mail included a letter from Mrs. Bernice Carlson requesting the identification of a bird she had heard singing. As the song came in through her open window, she duplicated it as best she could on the organ and sent me the score. Mrs. K. played it on our organ and we decided it was the white-throated sparrow. Was Mrs. Carlson pleased to learn that this exquisite songster of the north woods had paused in his migration to serenade at her window? Alas, no. She did so want it to be a meadowlark.

Birding is one of the fastest-growing forms of outdoor recreation, and it should be. It gets people out-of-doors and, unlike gardening or boating, it is a year-round hobby. It is free, requires no license, can be enjoyed in your own yard or even through your kitchen window or anywhere you happen to go. More advanced birders travel the world to add the names of birds to their life lists. It is a sport that combines well with everything from picnics to camping, fishing and vacationing. You can do it alone, with companions or in a group.

Only two pieces of equipment are needed to become a birder—a pair of binoculars and a book. The binoculars, most birders agree, should be either 6 or 7 power. Prices start at about $17, and most of the less expensive ones are quite satisfactory. If you wear glasses, be sure to get those which permit your eyes to get as close as possible to the back lenses.

The book should be an easily carried field guide, and in my opinion there is a choice of only two—*A Field Guide to the Birds* by Roger Tory Peterson, published by Houghton Mifflin Company, Boston, and *Birds of North America* by Robbins, Bruun and Zim, published by the Golden

Press, New York, $2.95. *Birds of North America,* a paperback, includes more species of birds, tells better where they can be found summer and winter, and charts their songs. The Peterson guide, a standard for many years, may be best for the beginner in this area because the birds of the West and the South are not included. It is thus easier to find the bird you are looking for, and it describes the groups of birds a little better, making it easier to find the proper page. However, both books are good and have excellent pictures.

Many people are frightened out of bird watching before they get started. In spring they go forth into the woods, fields and marshes and see hundreds of birds. They look into their field guide and see hundreds of birds. The task of matching them up appears frightening if not impossible. It is like the nonmusician looking first at the keys of the piano and then at a complicated musical score.

But bird watching really requires no schooling, no tutoring and, once a few tricks of the trade are learned, progress is rapid. However, like learning to swim, skate or play bridge, a little concentrated effort is required at the beginning.

It is not a matter of seeing a bird and then searching through the entire book until you find his picture. The birds that appear similar are grouped together in the guide so you learn distinctive characteristics of a bird to watch for and, having gone through your bird guide many times to become familiar with it, you quickly open it to the proper page.

For example, downy and hairy woodpeckers look very much alike. The hairy is larger but, not seeing them both at once, this doesn't help much. Opening your field guide to woodpeckers, you see them all on one page and note that the hairy has a proportionately larger bill. Bird number one is identified.

Before long, the instant your binoculars focus on a bird, your mind starts rapidly recording the details which will lead you to the right page—the shape of the bill; one bar on the wing, two or none; with or without eye rings; notched tail; relative size—like a sparrow, a robin, a crow. If it has a striped breast and a heavy bill, it is probably one of the many sparrows. A spot on the breast narrows down the identification.

Before long it becomes like speed reading. In an instant your mind records the color of the crown, throat, breast and back. A banded tail, white outer tail feathers or a white rump patch all stick in your memory long enough to locate your new find in the field guide.

Soon you learn also to take mental notes of a bird's actions and where it is found. A small nervous bird constantly flitting through the trees like a butterfly is probably a warbler. If he perches on a dead branch with clear vision all around, flies out to catch an insect and returns to his same perch, he is probably a flycatcher.

A bird hopping up the trunk of a tree is undoubtedly a woodpecker or a brown creeper. If he goes down the trunk head first, you can bet he is a nuthatch. Woodpeckers have an undulating flight made of several fast wing beats, then coasting with nearly closed wings. Swallows fly like— well, like only swallows can fly. But if it flies like a swallow and doesn't have a tail, it's a chimney swift.

It doesn't take long to learn that bluebirds, meadowlarks and bobo- links are found in open fields; that fox sparrows are usually scratching in dry leaves; that brown thrashers sing from treetops and catbirds from a clump of brush.

Hawks are a lot of fun and are divided into several groups: broad- winged buteos soar overhead; seldom-seen coopers and sharpshins dart through woods in pursuit of birds; little reddish sparrow hawks sit on wires; the pointed-winged long-tailed marsh hawk with the white rump patch soars low over fields.

If you are going to be a bird watcher, be particular. Distinguishing between swallows, hawks and sparrows is not a very gratifying achieve- ment. There are some twenty species of sparrows in this area. Which one is it? Incidentally, sparrows, warblers and shorebirds are probably the most difficult groups to learn and some of them, the warblers in particular, look different in the fall than they do in the spring. I think warblers were designed to deflate the ego of birders.

There was a time when birders themselves were considered a rather weird species. Birding was considered something less than a manly sport. But as increasing numbers of people, including some quite virile males, have become hooked on the hobby, the characterization of the typical birder seems to have been forgotten.

In addition to the obvious pleasures, birding can be an exciting avo- cation akin to hunting. There is the thrill of the chase sans shooting. For many, checking off another bird on the identification list is more gratifying than bringing one home in the game pocket. Unfortunately, the birder seldom understands the hunter unless he is one.

Before you have long been a birder, if you live in the Upper Midwest, you will want two more books. Both are inexpensive (25 cents each) and both can be obtained from the Bell Museum of Natural History, University of Minnesota, Minneapolis, Minn. The first is *Birds of the Minneapolis-St. Paul Region.* This includes a list of 285 species of birds in the area with spaces to check them off as you identify them. It tells you in what type of habitat each bird should be found, and the migration chart shows what time of year they are most likely to be seen. These dates and species may vary somewhat at a distance from the Twin Cities but are still very useful.

The second book is *Cultivating Your Garden Birds* by Dr. W. J. Breckenridge and Dr. D. W. Warner. In this booklet you can learn much about building birdhouses of various kinds, attracting birds to your yard, where to locate houses, what nesting material to provide, construction of birdbaths and even how to discourage sparrows.

Someday you may even want to get into bird photography or the more intricate and interesting fields of advanced bird study. You learn not only their life histories, but their relationship to other birds and to their environment—ecology. To sum it all up, birding can be as intriguing and time-consuming as you will let it. It is an incurable disease but quite a delightful one.

Flying Fly Traps

(Swallows)

It is bragging, I suppose, but on our back lot we claim to have one of the most expensive birdhouses in the country. Actually, this birdhouse is a worthless old shed on the edge of a swamp, but according to our tax statement it has a market value of about $400. We would like to burn the shed down and save $13 a year in taxes, but this would deprive the tenants of a summer home. These tenants which, incidentally, are several years behind in their rent, are a pair of barn swallows.

Most people who like birds have a favorite, and this favorite is apt to be the first bird they ever got to know. For me, this is the barn swallow.

My first childhood memories are of sitting at the edge of the wide-open doors of the barn watching these graceful birds dart in and out with balls of mud and pieces of grass which they somehow managed to plaster onto the vertical surface of the rafters to form a nest. Later I would watch as they fed their young, and finally I would see the babies take off in flight.

When I wasn't watching the barn swallows, our large gray cat was. She would crouch, apparently asleep, in the middle of the doorway and the annoyed swallows would dart back and forth over her head. Occasionally, one would come too low and the apparently sleeping cat would reach up and sometimes bring down a swallow.

There are over a hundred species of swallows in the world, but most of them are found in warmer climates. Only six species spend their summers in Minnesota. Of these, the barn swallow with its bright colors and long forked tail is probably the most beautiful. Swallows have small beaks but extremely wide mouths which open like insect nets for scooping their prey from the air. Being marvelous flyers, they spend most of their

Barn swallows—my nonpaying tenants

time on the wing. Nearly 100% of their food consists of insects caught in flight, the only exception being tree swallows which sometimes eat seeds and wild berries. Flies are the favorite food of barn swallows.

Apparently they originally nested on the rock faces of cliffs or caves, but since the coming of man they have become birds of the farm and use buildings with open doors or windows almost exclusively for their nesting. Both the male and the female take part in building the nest, hatching the eggs and rearing the young. Banding studies have shown that most of them return to nest in the same locality, if not the same barn, each year.

Swallows even bathe and drink while in flight by pausing momentarily over the water and dipping into it. They also pick insects off the surface of the water.

Once, while trout fishing on the Willow River in Wisconsin, I intently watched my dry fly as it floated down the riffle into a pool. I hoped a big brown trout would come up from the depths of the pool and take the bait. No big fish came up but, to my amazement, a small bird came down, picked up the fly and started off with it. The bird was one of a colony of bank swallows nesting nearby and, though several picked up the fly, they never got hooked.

Swallows in general are sociable birds which migrate together in vast mixed flocks. They do not appear to set up and defend territories as many other birds do. In fact, martins, bank swallows and cliff swallows nest in colonies.

It has been written that swallows are one of the most beneficial of all birds, never causing trouble or financial loss to man. But, of course, this is not true, for I continue to pay taxes on my worthless shed.

The Strange One

(Woodcock)

Woodcocks are strange birds. So are woodcock hunters. In fact, the two—the woodcocks and the hunters, that is, are alike in some ways. Of course, the hunters don't have as long bills or eyes in the back of their heads. At least, not all of them do, but, like the woodcock, they are a most seclusive lot.

Should you make the social blunder of asking a woodcock hunter where he hunts, his reply will be something like, "Up in Pine County." Even if this is a true statement, which is quite unlikely, it is of no help because you must know exactly where in Pine County.

Nor would it do you any good to try to follow a woodcock hunter to his favorite shooting ground because he is a rear-view mirror watcher. Only when no car is in sight does he dart off the highway on some secluded logging road where his car will be well hidden.

There is nothing reprehensible about this evasive action of woodcock hunters. It is all part of the sport. After all, woodcocks are not terribly difficult to shoot, but finding their secluded haunts is a real art.

In a moment of weakness, one woodcock hunter confided in me his secret of finding the birds. He will be most put out that I pass it on to you, but I'll chance it.

Being of a scientific bent, this hunter first gets a soil map and locates the soils that have loam in them. Then he finds an area that is pastured so the cover is not too dense nor the grass too tall. Adding my own two cents' worth, it always helps if there are a few alder thickets about.

A dog is a valuable asset in woodcock hunting. Of course, at first he doesn't recognize woodcocks as being much different from robins or flickers, but after you shoot a couple, he can be convinced that they are not on the songbird list and joins in the game with you. In fact, it is claimed that dogs really prefer woodcock hunting to anything else because the little worm eater gives off such a strong odor that the dog doesn't have to strain his nose.

Now to the woodcocks themselves. In appearance, at least, they are even more strange than their pursuers. Looking at one, you wonder if some blunder was made in his design. He really looks like something that should be sent back to the drawing board. In a way, he looks like his cousin, the jack snipe, except that he has short round wings and a plumper body. One of his strangest pieces of equipment is his bill which is not only very long but is sort of flexible. With the base of the bill tightly closed, he can still open the end of it to take hold of something.

That something is nearly always an angleworm because these constitute 87% of his annual diet. He doesn't buzz around much in the daytime, but mornings and evenings and even during the night he finds spots where the earth is soft, pokes his bill deep into it and with the flexible tip he plucks earthworms. This leaves a lot of funny little holes in the earth which look as if they were made with a stick about half the size of a pencil. And this reminds me of another thing about being a woodcock hunter. You have to learn to find "probes and splatters." Probes are holes and splatters are white.

Even more peculiar than the woodcock's bill are his eyes which are placed very high and far back on his head. Because the eyes move independently of each other, he not only can see in a complete 360-degree circle, but has a good overlap in the rear which gives him binocular vision from behind. I guess he is just more interested in where he's been than where he's going. Strange as this may seem, it is no doubt a fine arrangement for watching out for predators while his bill is deep in the ground tussling with a cantankerous angleworm.

A woodcock may not look like much of a Beau Brummel, but come spring, he is an ardent lover. Possibly he figures that a bird which looks as ridiculous as he does needs to compensate with a big courtship show. In spring, a male selects a "peenting ground" where he struts around with his bill tucked under his breast and gives the "peenting" call which sounds something like a nighthawk. Then he takes off on his long spiraling flight which goes up and up and up for 200 to 300 feet. All the while the specially designed outer three feathers of his wings are making a pleasant twittering noise. At the pinnacle of his flight, he gives his true love song and comes zigzagging back to earth again where he hopes to find that Mama Woodcock has come to admire the show. All this takes place in early morning or late evening and it truly is a show worth watching.

There are those who consider the woodcock to be an epicurean delicacy. But delicate is hardly the adjective to describe the exceedingly gamey flavor of woodcock which is very good if you like it. And a woodcock is a peculiar bird to the very end. Even lying on your plate beside the mashed potatoes and the rutabagas, he looks like nothing else because the breast is dark meat and the legs are light.

Probes and splatters—woodcock

Lilliputians of the Bird World

(Hummingbirds)

Hummingbirds, the Lilliputians of the bird world, are never confused with other birds, but sometimes they are mistaken for insects. Their flight and behavior when hovering before flowers is quite similar to that of the hawk-moth and sphinx-moth.

Found only in the new world, there are several hundred kinds of hummingbirds, but only the ruby-throat spends its summer in the Upper Midwest.

Various kinds of hummingbird feeders are becoming almost as popular in summer as the winter bird feeding stations. Feeders may be hung very close to windows because, though tiny, hummingbirds are quite fearless.

Like no other bird, the hummers can fly forward, backward, sideways, up and down or stand motionless in air. This is largely due to their exceptionally powerful breast muscles which control the wing beats. In most birds, the muscles which raise the wings are only about one-tenth the strength of those which pull the wings downward. But in hummingbirds, the upstroke muscles are almost half as heavy as those which force the wings down.

Thus, the little bird can stand erect in mid-air with its wings twisting like a variable pitch propeller so that the upstroke as well as the downstroke propels him upward or in whichever direction he wishes to go.

The amount of energy burned by these extremely active birds is phenomenal. By comparison, a 170-pound man, expending energy at the rate of the hummer, would have to eat 285 pounds of hamburger a day. He would also have to evaporate twelve gallons of perspiration per hour in order to keep his skin temperature below the boiling point. The little hummers are so active by day that they "hibernate" or become torpid at night in order to conserve energy by greatly reducing their heartbeat and body temperature.

The ruby-throated hummingbird, which nests as far north as Alberta and Nova Scotia, winters in Mexico and Central America. How such a tiny bird could make this flight was the subject of much speculation. For a time it was assumed that these and other tiny birds must surely ride on the backs of larger birds, such as hawks, in order to cover the distance.

The ruby-throat, beating his wings 75 times a second, can travel about 30 miles an hour on the straightaway. The trip from Louisiana to the tip of Yucatan is 575 miles, a 10-hour flight in good weather for a hummer. Someone has calculated that this trip requires 2,700,000 wing beats. Only three-fortieths of an ounce of fat is required for fuel to make this trip. On taking off from one shore, the hummer weighs about one-fifth ounce and is down to one-eighth ounce, about the weight of a penny, when he arrives at the other shore. In migration, hummingbirds seldom fly more than 25 feet above the ground or water.

What the hummer lacks in size he seems to make up for in agility and courage. He has few enemies and will attack and drive off kingbirds, jays, hawks and even eagles. However, according to Dr. Thomas S. Roberts' writings in his *Birds of Minnesota,* hummingbirds have a healthy respect for bees.

Occasionally hummers will be caught by frogs, entangled in spider webs or stuck on thistles. But their greatest enemy appears to be late frost which kills flowers on which they are feeding. Without an ample food supply, these tiny, energetic birds starve quickly.

Migrating separately, the males precede the females by several days in the spring, and the adult males start south a month before the females and their young make the trip in the fall.

The nest of a ruby-throated hummingbird, an inch in diameter and an inch deep, is a remarkable structure which is glued with the bird's own saliva to a branch where it looks like a knot. It is held together with the silk of spiders and caterpillars, and its outer walls are coverd with lichens to make it appear almost identical with the branch on which it clings.

Within the nest two white eggs, the size of peas, are laid. And it is the female alone which hatches the eggs and feeds the young five times an hour by regurgitation.

It was once believed that hummers lived almost entirely on flower nectar, but it has now been discovered that they visit the flowers as much to collect the tiny insects there as to sip the sweet liquid. Using its long tongue like a straw, nectar is sipped not only from flowers but from sap exuding from maple trees. In fact, hummers have been seen following sapsuckers from tree to tree to sip the sweet syrup from holes made by the sapsuckers.

There is considerable disagreement over the best formula to be placed in hummingbird feeders. A solution made up of one part honey to three or four parts water is probably the most frequently used. But it has been found that honey sometimes harbors a fungus which swells hummingbirds' tongues and causes them to starve. So a sugar solution containing less than 20 percent sugar is considered by some bird feeders to be better. Others say that only honey provides the vitamins, minerals, etc., needed by the birds. But perhaps the hummers can get the necessary vitamins and proteins from the many insects they eat.

Just as the least shrew, the tiniest of all mammals, is the most active and will starve in eight hours without a meal, the smallest of birds, the hummingbird, is by far the most active and has a heart which beats 615 times per minute.

The ruby-throated hummingbird is a common resident throughout all parts of the Upper Midwest. It is found in the groves of the prairie region, the open glades of the forest and in yards everywhere flowers are to be found. Hummingbirds have been called the gems of the bird world, and Audubon describes them as "glittering fragments of the rainbow."

Peck Order

Peck order, that social hierarchy which permits dominant birds to lord it over the submissive ones, is familiar to everyone who has observed birds at the feeding station. Applying our human emotions to wild things, and we all do it to a degree, we tend to favor the underdog and resent the bully blue jay which rules the roost. But peck order may be essential to the survival of many species.

Our feeding station is being kept open for business this summer and proves as interesting to observe as during winter. Let's see how well you do on the following quiz.

Along with the lesser birds at our feeding station, there are grackles, blue jays, redheaded woodpeckers and, of course, squirrels. Can you arrange them in the proper peck order?

First of all, you may be a bit surprised that we have redheaded woodpeckers at our feeding station. Perhaps it is not uncommon, but I have not seen it before and thought the woodpeckers should be out plucking worms and beetles out of trees. But, at the present, they are the birds most frequently seen at the feeder and seem quite content with sunflower seeds.

As would be expected, the gray squirrel dominates the peck order. Among the birds, it was first the blue jays. Then came the grackles which gradually asserted their dominance over the jays. Before this order of supremacy was definitely established, the first redheaded woodpecker arrived. In the beginning, he was wary of both the jays and grackles and would back off the edge of the feeder somewhat as they approached.

Suddenly this changed. The woodpecker prefers aerial combat. I saw him dive into a flying jay and there was a burst of feathers—blue jay

89

feathers. Having established a superior position over the jays, the red-headed woodpeckers (several of them now) drove the grackles from the feeder. On one occasion we saw them dive-bombing the squirrel which would duck to the underside of the feeder at each attack. But he would never leave.

But the peck order is not yet finally established. Blue jays are definitely subordinate to both the redheaded woodpeckers and the grackles, but the grackles are now serious contenders for the number one position as we continue to watch the drama unfold from our ringside seat at the breakfast table.

Of course, peck order is established not only between species, but within many species of birds and mammals, including man, and even in some fishes and reptiles. Sometimes it prevails only during the mating season, but often it lasts throughout the year and throughout the life of an individual. Each wolf knows his place in the pack.

Baby chicks live amicably together, but within a few weeks fighting and bullying begin, and before two months have passed the order of dominance has been well established from alpha to omega. Alpha has earned the right to lord it over any other chicken in the flock. Beta may peck any chicken except Alpha. And so on down the line to poor Omega with no one to peck.

This system might seem to lead to endless fighting which would detract from the more serious business of finding a living and producing young. Actually, the reverse is true. Once the hierarchy is established, each individual knows his place and the fighting is virtually over. A threatening posture from Alpha is all that is needed to assert his dominance in every activity from feeding to mating. There appears to be truth in the old proverb, "Only the brave deserve the fair."

Occasionally the peck order may not lie in a straight line from Alpha to Omega. A triangle may develop where Alpha can peck Beta and Beta can peck Gamma but Gamma can peck Alpha. Such triangles, or even polygons, are not uncommon in our own society.

To the human observer, all birds of a species look alike and we wonder if they can really tell each other apart. The establishment of the peck order proves they can because it can be maintained only when each member of the flock recognizes and remembers each of the other individuals. In one experiment it was determined that a domestic hen could distinguish twenty-seven others in four different flocks.

Scientists conducted further experiments to determine if it were actual recognition or something else which taught each individual his position in life. They altered the appearance of hens by placing bonnets over their combs, dying feathers, etc. The hens so altered were at once treated as strangers by the rest of the flock and had to fight to reestablish their positions in the peck order.

Scientists have learned that the ability to win fights is not the sole criteria in establishing a position in the peck order. Appearance and general behavior play a part, and with some species territory is important. It is well known that a dog fights best in his own yard. A cock pheasant will drive an invading cock out of his territory, only to be driven back himself by the same cock when he gets into his territory. Psychological as well as physical factors seem to be involved. This was recognized nearly twenty centuries ago by Seneca who said, "The cock is at his best on his own dung hill."

As a rule, males dominate the females, but this is sometimes reversed during the nesting season. When experimenters dyed the feathers of the females to make them look like males, they attained dominance over the other females.

One characteristic of peck order involves the altered social status at the selection of a mate. When a high-ranking male chooses a female of low rank for his mate, the wife immediately takes on the status of her husband. Of course, this never occurs in the species homo sapiens.

Bird Compasses

(Migration)

Migration, that ability of birds and some other animals to unerringly travel the globe, has baffled man since the dawn of reason. But there are rays of light.

A German ornithologist, Gustav Kramer, put warblers into a circular cage open at the top so the birds could see only the sky. The cage had a transparent floor so Kramer could lie underneath at night and watch his birds. When the birds had the urge to migrate, Kramer observed that, with only the sky in view, they oriented themselves north in spring and south in fall. Kramer also discovered that when the skies were overcast, the headings of his birds were entirely disrupted. This strongly indicated that birds are celestial navigators and have no built-in compasses or "sense of direction" such as men like to ascribe to their favorite Indian guides.

Then Franz Sauer, at the University of Freiburg, conducted similar experiments with a circular cage but, in addition to the natural sky, he got the same results in a planetarium where he could imitate the appearance of sky at some other place on the earth's surface. The warblers looked at the artificial sky and headed in the right direction.

Sauer also used adult warblers which had been raised indoors, had never seen the sky and were, therefore, totally inexperienced. These, too, headed in the right direction when they looked at the sky. Many scientists have found this hard to believe because it implies that migrating birds have some mechanism built into their brains which causes them to react to the pattern of the stars in a specific way.

Scientists believe that birds have two separate and distinct methods of orientation. The first, which man finds easiest to understand, is called "directional orientation" which means they have the ability to select the proper compass direction. This is probably accomplished by observing the stars, sun and moon.

The second, which still appears to have man almost totally baffled, is called "goal-directed orientation." An example of this is found in homing pigeons which can be moved in any direction and can find their way back to the loft. It has been demonstrated that other birds can do the same.

With a compass, map and a known point of beginning, man can travel anywhere. It appears that, through stellar observation, birds have the compass, but what they use in place of the map has scientists puzzled.

Another feature of migration which confuses scientists is the ability of birds to change direction during migration. Ducks from western and central Canada may migrate southeast, cutting across the normal waterfowl flyways until they reach the eastern flyway where they turn south.

In New England, two scientists transported common terns a considerable distance. When released, the terns consistently headed southeast, which was in the direction of their home. Then a second group of terns were released which should have headed northeast to reach home but, to the surprise and disappointment of the scientists, they, too, headed southeast. Here again, in both cases they noted that when skies were overcast, the terns flew off in all directions. But why they consistently fly southeast when their sky compass is visible remains an enigma.

Later, it was discovered that mallard ducks do much the same thing only in a different direction. They were taken off in several directions from the Slimbridge Waterfowl Research Station in England to determine if they would fly directly back to their home. Much to the surprise of the scientists, the mallards always flew northwest regardless of where they were released. A similar experiment was carried out with mallards by Frank Bellrose in Illinois. His mallards always headed north, and again, in both England and Illinois, the released ducks scattered at random when the skies were overcast.

This inclination of certain birds to always fly in a certain direction has been called "nonsense orientation." It may serve some good purpose, but no one understands what. One theory is that disturbed birds will always fly in a certain direction in order for them to again reassemble in a flock.

To determine if mallards would follow their same "nonsense orientation" at night, small lights were attached to their legs at both the England and Illinois experiments. Batteries were attached to the ducks' legs with soft paper which would melt and free the ducks of their cargoes when they landed in the water.

Once again, the England ducks headed northwest and the Illinois ducks north, indicating that the mallards could use stars as well as the sun for their compasses.

Hunters watching ducks enter and leave a refuge just before and after shooting hours jokingly say, "They must carry watches." They do. It has been well established that birds have surprisingly accurate biological clocks which tell them the time of day and time of year. To orient themselves by the sun, they have to know what time it is. By putting captive birds under artificial lights, their clocks are quite easily reset by regulating the lights.

This was done to several groups of mallards: one flock had its clocks set six hours ahead, another six hours late; a third group was shifted twelve hours out of phase and the final control group was kept outdoors under natural daylight and darkness.

When released on a clear day, the several groups of mallards headed in different directions in accordance with the resetting of their clocks. Those with their biological clocks six hours ahead behaved as if it were six hours later in the day and flew off to the southwest thinking they were going northwest. The mallards which had been put twelve hours out of phase headed southeast instead of northwest.

However, when these birds with their clocks reset were released under the stars, all of them headed northwest. Resetting their internal timing mechanism had thrown their sun compass out of kilter but they were still able to orient themselves accurately by the stars.

Attracting Birds

Whoever established the "wet hen" as the criteria for something to be madder than had obviously never encountered a mother with a young son who she felt had been wronged, cheated or discriminated against. I had a call from one such indignant mother, and what she was mad at was the birds.

She explained that her son had built a bird-feeding station, set it out, stocked it with food, and the birds refused to come. When I learned the station had only been out two days I tried to explain that sometimes it took a little longer, but she assured me that two days were a long time for a small boy to wait, and he was most disappointed. After listening to this lady for awhile, I could not understand how even a bird would dare disappoint her son. But, following a few questions, I learned that none of the neighbors had bird feeders and, because it was a new housing development, there were no trees or shrubs in the vicinity. I am sure my attempts to explain the situation did not alter her opinion that her son was being robbed of his inalienable rights to have birds at his new feeding station.

It is quite important to get bird-feeding stations started early in the fall because many species such as chickadees, nuthatches, downy and hairy woodpeckers, blue jays and cardinals do not appear to move much after they have established winter quarters. On the other hand, everyone who feeds birds knows that evening grosbeaks, cedar waxwings, Bohemian waxwings, crossbills and purple finches may show up at any time during the winter and, if they find food to their liking, stay.

The placing of feeders is important. We have found that to attract the most birds, a feeder should not be too close to the house, but, of course, to see them best you can't beat a bird feeder right on the windowsill. So,

Evening Grosbeaks

like many people, we have two bird feeders, one out in the yard and one on the windowsill. This way chickadees and nuthatches have dinner with us. Our table is next to the inside of the window, theirs on the outside.

A variety of food is good for a variety of birds. Of course, they eat the sunflower seeds first because they are the more expensive. But many of them hang on the suet bag, and chickadees in particular appear to enjoy picking peanut butter out of holes drilled in a stick of wood. Some people mix bacon fat with peanut butter, but this could be dangerous because it is salty. Birds apparently like salt, but it will kill them quite easily if they do not have a ready supply of water.

Feeders which are maintained in the same place year after year attract more birds, indicating that the birds do actually remember where last year's winter food supply was. Dr. Breckenridge, director of the Bell Museum of Natural History, did not have his hummingbird feeder out one spring before the hummingbird returned. To his surprise the hummingbird hovered about the window in the exact location where the feeder had been the previous year.

Remember that feeding birds carries an obligation. You probably aren't saving the lives of many, if any, songbirds by feeding them, but you are attracting them in close for your enjoyment. However, once they have established the habit of feeding in one place they may be in serious trouble if you stop feeding, unless, of course, your neighbors are feeding them. This sometimes happens when people take winter vacations in February or March.

Frequently the most critical period for our winter birds is during spring ice storms in late March or April. When sheets of ice cover everything for two days or more, many birds will die. Feeding at this time can save them.

Of course, the amount of trees, shrubs and vines in your yard and in your neighborhood influence the number of birds that will winter there. This is not exactly the season to be planting shrubs, but if you are interested in planning for more birds, you might order a copy of *Cultivating Your Garden Birds* for 35 cents from the Bell Museum of Natural History, University of Minnesota, Minneapolis. It contains some interesting ideas for birdhouses, feeders, trees and shrubs to be planted, etc. A second booklet available from the same source for 25 cents is called *Birds of the Minneapolis-St. Paul Region.* This is primarily a check list showing which species of birds is most likely to be in the Twin City area at every month of the year.

Dr. Breckenridge is predicting that this will be a winter when we will see snowy owls, and several have already been reported. Every fourth year when the lemming population of the far north hits the low of its cycle, snowy owls move south in search of food.

Birds at the feeding station bring winter cheer and delight to young and old in countless families. Many homes would give up the TV set ahead of the feeding station. Bird feeding is a source of pleasure which some families would not sell at any price, but the impatient mother of the disappointed boy could neither command nor buy it. It is one of life's pleasures which cannot be bought or sold. It can only be earned.

Stoking the Feathered Furnace

This being New Year's Day, you will probably eat too much, but that chickadee cracking sunflower seeds on your bird feeder must consume a great deal more food in proportion to his size than you do or he would not survive until tomorrow morning. This is not only because he is probably going to have a much more active day than you are, but he must convert a lot of carbohydrates into heat.

In winter, birds are like little stoves, and the lower the temperature the more fuel they must shovel in.

House sparrows cannot survive in the far north because they cannot eat enough food to keep them alive overnight. At 71 degrees below zero a house sparrow could survive only four hours without food. At 64 below he still could not survive the 14½ hours which is the average length of a winter's night in the temperate zone. At 57 degrees below zero he can survive a maximum of 19 hours without food.

Hungry birds can survive the longest, 67 hours, when the temperature is 84 degrees. Food requirements increase as the temperature either rises or falls. At 102 degrees a fasting sparrow can survive only 14 hours.

All animals are either cold-blooded or warm-blooded and, if you want a couple of new words for your vocabulary, these are called "poikilothermic" or "homoiothermic."

The cold-blooded animals, such as fish, amphibians and reptiles, have a body temperature approximately the same as their environment and it rises and falls with the surrounding temperature.

Only mammals and birds are warm-blooded and maintain a relatively constant body temperature. Being warm-blooded has many advantages, including that of being able to live in cold climates.

Birds have higher and more variable temperatures than mammals and, interestingly enough, the more primitive types of birds have lower temperatures than modern birds. The kiwi, for example, has a body temperature of 100 degrees, which is 11 or 12 degrees lower than that of the house sparrow.

If man's body temperature rises two or three degrees he is terribly sick, but it is customary for the house wren's temperature to fluctuate 14 degrees throughout a 24-hour day. Usually the smaller the bird the higher his temperature, and the tiny body inside of that fluff of chickadee feathers you are looking at has a temperature of about 114 degrees.

It is hard to understand how such a tiny stove could contain enough fuel to keep burning through a long, cold winter night. A sparrow with an empty stomach cannot survive if his body temperature drops below 91 degrees.

Yet, by consuming a lot of food and a lot of oxygen, birds do some amazing things. The Emperor penguin breeds in Arctic temperatures of 80 degrees below zero. This is considered one of the most remarkable physiological feats among warm-blooded animals.

Consuming an abundance of oxygen and food, the hummingbird has a metabolism 12 times that of a pigeon, 25 times that of a chicken and 100 times that of an elephant. If an elephant's metabolism were as rapid as that of a hummingbird, he would literally cook himself to death.

It would appear that hummingbirds and shrews have theoretically reached the smallest size possible for warm-blooded animals. If they got any smaller they would probably not be able to eat food fast enough to avoid starvation.

I have always wondered how birds kept their tiny feet from freezing, and it is true that these unfeathered parts account for much heat loss. While standing with legs exposed, the domestic fowl loses 40 percent to 50 percent more heat than while sitting. And tucking her head under her wing reduces heat loss by another 12 percent.

Apparently when the legs and feet are exposed they are kept from freezing by pumping a lot of blood through them. A chickadee's heart beats at the rate of ten times per second.

Even if their feet do get a bit cold, they still function, because birds discovered the value of winter lubricants a few million years ahead of

Chickadee eating peanut butter

automotive engineers. The fatty oils which lubricate the joints and tendons in bird's legs and feet have a very low solidifying point. In other words, it will remain fluid at much lower temperatures than normal body fats.

Don't forget that the birds you have enticed in to entertain you at the bird feeder have become dependent on you for the vast quantities of food they need in cold weather. Have a neighbor keep the bird feeders filled if you migrate south for a winter vacation.

Prairie Chickens

It has been a long search, but I have finally located one who agrees with me when I talk about prairie chickens. What I have read in books he has seen firsthand.

M. E. Isherwood has lived in Sebeka, fourteen miles north of Wadena, Minnesota, for a long time. In fact, he has been publisher of the Sebeka Review for fifty-eight years. Seventy-eight years ago he was born in Jackson County, Minnesota, and moved north with his family in a covered wagon when he was nine years old. His father was the first mayor of Sebeka.

When Mr. Isherwood started talking about the good old days of prairie chicken hunting I said, "But prairie chickens were not native to Minnesota when the white man first came here." On every other occasion when I have made this remark I have ended up in an argument with someone who tells me about wagonloads of prairie chickens his grandfather used to shoot. But Mr. Isherwood said, "That's right. When I first came here there was no farming and practically no prairie chickens. In fact, they did not become abundant until about the turn of the century when we had quite a few settlers. Then, by 1910 or so, when the land was all taken up and being farmed, the prairie chicken started to decline."

The prairie chicken story is perhaps the best example we have of how completely dependent any wild species is on his environment. Minnesota, Wisconsin, the Dakotas, and even Iowa and Nebraska were not the native habitat of the prairie chicken which lived further south. The sharp-tailed grouse were always here, but the early explorers never found chickens.

Prairie chickens have two major habitat requirements—a large acreage of native grassland and a few small food patches. In the northern states the grasslands were abundant but food was inadequate. It was the early settlers who changed the environment to the liking of the chickens. The farmer, his plow and his cow migrated into the prairies and cultivated small patches of grain. The limiting factor of a deficient food supply was gone. The chickens migrated north and west and for a time were extremely abundant. They were not only hunted for food and sport but market hunters took them in great numbers and they were shipped to eastern markets from the rail centers at Sioux Falls and Sioux City.

Now, although the hunting season has long been closed, prairie chickens are found in only a few isolated places in the northern states. Ask anyone what happened to them and he will tell you that the market hunters got them and what they didn't get the sportsmen finished off. But the fact is, as Mr. Isherwood could testify, it was not the shotgun, but the plow and the cow which depleted the prairie chicken. Interestingly enough, the plow and the cow which brought them there later became the instruments of their destruction, and if there had never been a market hunter or a 12-gauge shotgun, the number of prairie chickens remaining in these states today would be virtually the same.

At first the chickens could not live here because of an inadequate food supply. Now the food is plentiful but the abundance of native grass which they require is gone. As Mr. Isherwood remembers, their numbers declined as farmers turned the better soils with the plow and mowed the native grass to provide hay for their growing dairy herds.

In *Birds of Minnesota,* Dr. Thomas S. Roberts estimated that prairie chickens became established in Minnesota before 1850, and Mr. Isherwood remembers the stories his father used to tell about hunting chickens on horseback in Jackson County a long, long time ago.

One thing still confusing me is the fact that old-timers always speak of the prairie chickens as "yellow legs" in contrast to the sharp-tailed grouse with feathers on their legs. I have seen, studied and photographed prairie chickens in Nebraska, South Dakota and Minnesota and they all have feathers on their legs. I can only guess that because in the old days most of the chicken hunting was probably done in August, the birds may not have had feathers on their legs at that time. I seriously doubt that after living many generations in this northern climate they have developed feather stockings which they did not have before.

Is there anything we could do to make the prairie chicken once more abundant in Minnesota? Yes, but we're not likely to do it. If we would let much of our natural prairie go back to native grass, chickens would increase, but at the expense of farmers. We still have chickens in limited areas. In fact, there is one concentration of over 200 near Sebeka. It is there because a large area of marsh grass is seldom cut for hay.

In talking about days of prairie chicken abundance and hunting them over a good bird dog, Mr. Isherwood reminisced, "Boy, we had fun in those days!" Prairie chickens have added an interesting chapter to our history. They should also have taught us that every living thing, including man, thrives or declines according to the abundance of his natural environment.

We Shook On It

Did you ever shake hands with your son—seriously, I mean? I did last week in a duck blind. It's an experience you won't forget. What did we shake hands on? I'll tell you in a minute, but before that we must have the setting.

First there was the drive north in the beautiful tag end of autumn. Then the companionship of an evening in a cabin which we designed and built ourselves. In the morning, while waiting for the noon opening of the duck season, we sat on an island in the marsh testing our skill with binoculars and the waterfowl identification book. Next came blind-building and the setting of the decoys.

This done, we poured our first cups of coffee from the thermos bottle and placed idle, never-to-be-paid wagers on who would shoot the first duck, the most ducks, and who would use the least shells in doing it.

As we chatted, a pair of dragonflies, attached in tandem, flew over the water. It was interesting to know that the male was helping the female to deposit her eggs. Each time they touched the surface of the water she deposited a few eggs and he, being in front, helped to lift her quickly from the water before she could become a tasty morsel for a lurking bass.

Blackbirds, behaving more like a swarm than a flock, passed close above our heads. The funny round head and flat face of a muskrat popped out of the water beside our blind, and he stared with his beady eyes before submerging more in disgust than in fear.

The marsh stank, and it was a delightful stink—reminiscent of the countless hours we have spent in duck blinds. It was then, before we had seen a duck or fired a shot, that we vowed we would spend at least one

Son David Kimball

fall day a year together on the marsh even though the duck season be closed. We shook on it.

The appointed hour at last arrived and our guns were loaded. Nostalgic complacency gave way to watchful anticipation. "Mark east! A pair of mallards!" But they swung wide. We heard the faint whistle of evenly beating wings, and we knew before we spotted them that this flock would be high.

Then we heard the erratic swishing and popping of wings, a sound created only by the twisting and turning contortions of ducks as they dive in from high altitudes, a sound familiar only to duck hunters.

An hour passed and we had not fired a shot. Then son David said excitedly, "Look north, Pa!"

At first I saw nothing. Then one thin line. Then many more. And within a minute the air overhead was literally filled with ducks.

We missed and we hit. With a limit of one each, the shooting of mallards was soon over. We tried to finish out with a pair of bluebills, but somehow a greenwing teal, the littlest duck of all, was shot.

Four ducks for two hunters. Not much shooting, but a day filled with companionship, nostalgia, anticipation, excitement and drama. A day in a world apart—a world without typewriters, traffic, TV or telephones.

Then the hospitality of the cabin. The fire to warm our backsides. And when we closed our eyes we saw the ducks still flying. They came in singles, in pairs and in flocks, but just for a little while. We needed no sleeping pills that night.

Classifying Hunters

The variety of game to be found in Minnesota is exceeded only by the diversity of hunters pursuing it. With a little practice, you can learn to classify hunters—cataloging them by species, subspecies, and variety.

First, and easiest to identify, is the "game getter." His sole purpose in being out is to shoot something. His gun, always of the largest caliber, is firmly clenched in both hands as his watchful eyes search only for game. His stride is direct and determined—the same stride he uses between the First National Bank and the brokerage office. When he spots you approaching on the trail, his expression changes from one of eager determination to annoyance. He is sure you are a clumsy idiot who has frightened all the game out of the country. When you meet on the trail, he nods and possibly even grunts a little. Be content with it. This is more recognition than you would be accorded had you met him on Hennepin Avenue.

Another type, easily classified, is the "prone hunter." Though relatively abundant in cabins, this species is somewhat of a rarity in the woods. However, should you get in the proximity of one you will certainly be aware of his presence. Seldom found in an upright position, he usually reclines on the sunny side of a hill. Invariably he will be surrounded by candy wrappers, bits of lunch paper, empty cigarette packs, and a thermos bottle. Oh, yes, he also has a gun, a fine polished weapon, unscratched and always out of reach. Frequently he will have a crude bonfire in front of him which produces little heat but great volumes of stinking smoke. Likely he will never see you as you walk past, but if he does, you may be sure he will immediately shout some greeting like, "How's luck?" or "Have you seen any?" Why this species always shouts has not, to my knowledge, been scientifically determined. Not being noted for bravery afield, it is possible the "prone hunter" does this to avoid being mistaken for some other species which may be legally harvested. If you are lost, a "prone hunter" is one of the finest signs in the woods. When you see one, you can be sure you are not more than a hundred yards from a cabin or a car.

About one in twenty-five deer hunters is "arboreal" in nature. Some build platforms in trees that look like crude beginnings of tree houses. This is legal if not over six feet from the ground. The more rugged ones climb high into trees, pulling their guns after them on a rope. Of course, a few get shot down in the process and some fall, but it is really death from freezing that prevents this species from becoming more abundant.

Inadvertently, I once nearly caused the undoing of an "arboreal hunter." He was high in a maple right on a refuge boundary. Walking by, I shouted, "What would you do if you saw a deer in the refuge?"

Answer: "I'd shoot the so and so."

A few minutes later my partner walked in behind me and the ape man said, "Who was that guy ahead of you?"

Answer: "The State Director of Game and Fish!"

Our "arboreal hunter" narrowly escaped a nasty fall.

One of our most successful deer hunters is the "stump sitter." These hunters have one characteristic in common—always fat. Here we should not confuse cause and effect. They are not stump sitters because they are fat. They are fat because they are, by nature, stump sitters.

No research has been done on this species, but it is believed that more than fifty percent of them shoot deer. It can, therefore, be concluded that more than half of them have the sagacity and stamina to sit facing the wind. Even the "stump sitter" can be detected by the keen nose of a deer if he is upwind.

The exact opposite of the "stump sitter" is the "hyperthyroid hunter." Lean, wiry, eager, and nervous, he constantly drives or stalks. He knows that standing still is one of the best ways to hunt, and he tries, but he can't. He takes a stand but soon decides it is not a good location because he can't see enough. So, in five minutes he is off looking for a new stand.

These "hyperthyroids" are a boon to all patient hunters. Without their constant movement, few deer would run past the "stump sitters."

The "local deer hunter" can be identified by his clothes, his gun, and his good nature. His more or less red outfit looked better before he used it while cutting pulpwood last winter. His 30-30 lever-action rifle with open iron sights is old and well worn, and he always has plenty of time to sit and talk a spell. A strange thing about this species is that they are frequently seen dragging deer out of the woods.

Of course, there are other species hardly worthy of mention. One would be the "cabin sitter." He will occasionally "sit out a hand" and look out of the cabin windows. He once heard of a man who got a deer that way. Thereupon he resolutely decided to adopt this hunting technique.

There must be one species of hunter which has not been described because surely none of these descriptions fit me. They don't fit you either, do they?

On Training a Wife

Equal rights for men and women are something I'm for. Of course, there must be some division of duties according to well-established custom. For example, it is as normal for a man to go hunting and fishing as it is for a women to have babies—and that is a fair division of labor.

Back in 1920 we passed the woman's suffrage amendment, but all that did was increase the woman's vote to two—one for herself in addition to the one she instructed her husband to make.

We think we have perfected about the ultimate in a civilization, but I'm not so sure. Consider the Indian civilization before the white man came in and messed it up. The brave would go out and kill some game or catch some fish and he would even drag it home himself if it weren't too heavy. Then, while he curled up in his tepee for a well-earned nap, his squaw would dress and clean the game, cook it, smoke it, make jerky and such. I can't for the life of me see how we think we have replaced that fine arrangement with a superior civilization. Our forefathers should have their pictures turned to the wall for not adopting some of those fine old Indian customs.

Of course, I am for true equal rights for the sexes, and Indians didn't have this in every respect. For example, when an Indian took his squaw out in the woods, she had to walk three steps behind him. That's no good for us. In the first place, she might shoot you in the back, and in the second place, she is no good to you there. Get her out in front where she might flush some game.

Nowadays, when a man comes home from a long hard day on the lake and throws a string of fish in the sink, some wives actually have the

Mrs. K. on snowshoes

audacity to say, "You caught 'em, you clean 'em!" Is that a fair division of labor? When a man brings home a pay check I never heard of a woman saying, "You earned it, you spend it!"

I don't know how we men let ourselves be beguiled into this totally inequitable misconception that dressing game and cleaning fish is a man's job. By all that is just and right, it is woman's work. But now that the precedent has been established, it is going to take a full generation to set things right again, and we had best be at it.

There is not much hope for the present generation of women, so the first responsibility falls on you fathers of girls. You must start right now and teach your daughters to dress game and clean fish.

Take my father-in-law for instance. Bless him, there was a man who knew how to bring up a daughter. When I visited their cabin on Kabe-cona Lake and saw that girl fillet a walleye, it was love at first sight. And

Ken Black, on left, went fishing.

when she beat me at picking ducks, I went and bought the ring. Smartest move I ever made.

Of course, if your woman "warn't broke" right, the situation "ain't" entirely hopeless. I've heard of some coming around with hardly any beating at all. Some fellows trick their wives into it by taking them hunting and getting them to shoot something. It is not always easy to find a bird that will fly into their wild shots, but if you can kill a bird the same instant they shoot and then swear you never pulled a trigger, you've got it made. When you get home, just use her own words and say, "You shot it, you dress it." Getting her to clean one is the big first step. When a woman shudders and says, "Ish! I couldn't touch the bloody or slimy thing," she isn't being squeamish, she's being smart.

Another thing about taking her hunting is that she will find out just how pooped a hunter gets. Next time you come home from a hunt, she will know just how much you need to curl up in your tepee and take a nap.

Some fellows tell me that after leaving their wives home while they go fishing every weekend for a couple of months, these wives get a little uncooperative.

One time we had a fine fishing trip lined up, and Ken Black found himself in this predicament. Ken is really a hunter. He hates fishing but he loves fishing trips.

Anyway, Ken hadn't been home for a good many weekends and was a bit concerned about what sort of a fuss Marge would put up if he started packing his gear again. But the more we talked about the trip the better it sounded, and Ken finally said he would go. A little doubtful about his ability to get around Marge, we asked how he would work it.

"I don't use it too often," he said, "but I've got one trick that never fails. When I get home, instead of sitting in the living room reading the paper, I'll perch on a chair in the kitchen where Marge is making dinner and just sit there with my chin in my hands, saying nothing. Pretty soon she will say, 'What's the matter, Ken?' and I'll say, 'Nothin'.' A little later she will ask, 'Are you sick?' and I'll say, 'No, don't think so.' Then, after awhile she'll say, 'What are you thinking about?' Then I'll tell her that you fellows asked me to go on this wonderful fishing trip but, of course, I told them that I couldn't go because I have been away from home so much lately.

"Well, about the time we have finished dinner and I have left half the food on my plate, Marge will say, 'Could you still go if you called them now?' "

It was a good fishing trip and Ken was there. But isn't it a shame that the modern male has become so downtrodden and his stature so degraded in modern society that he must resort to such trickery to continue those manly activities which are his birthright?

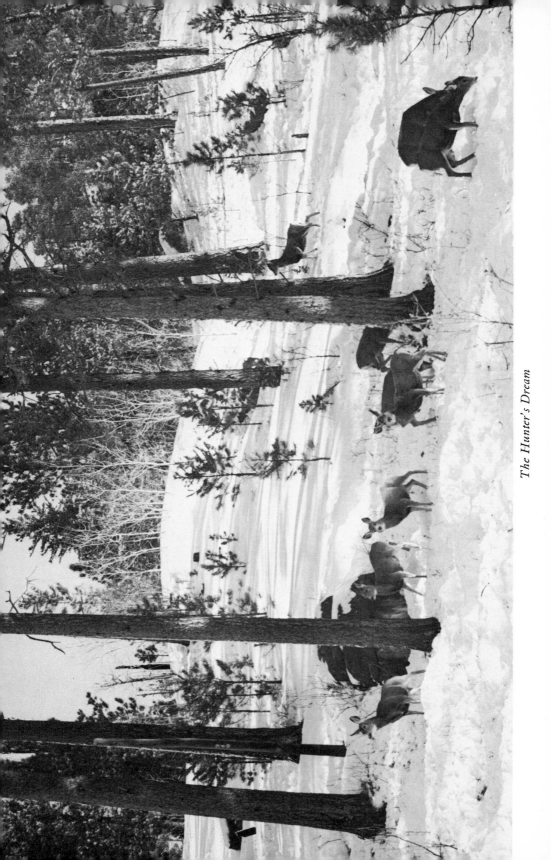

The Hunter's Dream

Meditations on a Deer Stand

What is a deer's best friend? Could it be this smelly pipe in my mouth? Smoking may cause heart attacks among men, but it has warned many a deer against an attack on his heart. Or could it be the mothballs dear wife packed my hunting coat in, or the fact that I didn't take a shower this morning?

While these odors of man have saved the lives of a multitude of wary deer, probably none would rank as the number one danger warning. I'm facing upwind and, besides, a deer's weapons of defense are probably 80% ears, 19% nose and 1% eyes.

The common cold of man may well be the deer's best friend. One cough, sneeze or blow every five minutes is all the warning he needs. The clicking of loose cartridges in a pocket, noisy canvas pants or even the crunching of a crisp apple are all sounds which have befriended deer.

Or how about that red squirrel scolding me, or the squawking jay? Does my quarry know their language, too?

Oh, dandy! Here comes another friendly hunter. How long will he stand and chat? I like friendly hunters. Sometimes they have good advice, but I suspect their gregarious nature has benefited more deer than men.

Well, he didn't stay too long. What were we thinking about? Oh, yes—the deer's best friend. What about the mental traits and physical prowess of his pursuer—man? The restless, impatient nature of man certainly contributes to the longevity of deer as do his weak peripheral vision, relatively poor hearing and near absence of smell.

It occurs to me that this notebook and pen may be the deer's best friend as far as this hunter is concerned. I had better rise from this comfortable log seat and look for awhile.

Deer Fawn

Later

Now, from personal experience I can authentically report two new scientific facts. First, writing in a notebook with a ball-point pen does not make sufficient noise to frighten deer. Second, the safety catch on some modern rifles is the deer's best friend and the hunter's worst enemy.

As I looked around there was a movement. It approached, and as it passed through the heavy timber and brush I got a momentary glimpse of a fine big buck. He came toward the old woods road as I hoped he would and, just as he was about to step into the open, I threw up my gun and pushed the safety button—"CLICK!"

At the sound, he tensed and froze for a second. Only a hunter knows how many pages of thought go through a man's mind in one such second.

In my scope was the west half of a deer headed east. A shot through the hams would bring him down, but spoiling so much meat would be unforgivable. Besides, how could I explain to companions such an ill-placed bullet in a standing deer? I aimed at the trees which concealed his front half. Would a bullet penetrate those trees? Not likely. Then the cross hairs were on the spine just ahead of the rump—the best part of the deer. But I could spare a few chops. The cross hairs wavered a bit and a miss of a few inches could mean a "gut shot" deer and no trailing snow. He was too noble an animal for this. I would wait until he took one more step.

A flash of his white tail and he was gone. Back in the brush, he snorted five times—louder and more defiantly than I have ever heard a deer snort before.

Now some of you are sure to write and tell me that the safety on my Remington model 740 can be released quietly if I grasp it between thumb and forefinger and ease it over.

I know, friend, I know. That is what I did last fall, with success. But after hunting grouse, pheasants and ducks for a couple of months, I forgot.

The man who invented the noisy safety may be a friend of the deer but not of the hunter. Of course, for we hunters who failed, he did provide an excuse—however feeble.

Avoiding Bullets and Heart Attacks

Many heart attacks and hunting accidents can be prevented. Sportsmen will soon start to enjoy another deer season. Unfortuantely, a few will not return.

Some will be shot and probably more will suffer heart attacks. Considering that there may be a quarter of a million hunters, the chance that this will happen to any one of them is slight. But this makes the losses no less tragic, especially when most of them, both the shootings and the heart attacks, could be avoided.

We won't burden you with a lot of do's and don'ts about safe hunting which few would read and even fewer would remember. Our one recommendation is that you wear a blaze-orange cap. A blaze-orange vest is highly desirable, too—but especially get the cap. In tests throughout the country it has been proved that blaze orange, the most unnatural color in nature, is far superior to red. In fact, red has been proved a relatively poor color.

However, many hunters won't get around to buying new caps, so I am going to make a suggestion to wives and mothers. Throw out your husband's or son's old red cap and buy him the most brilliant blaze-orange cap you can find. A couple of dollars is cheap insurance, especially when you are buying the kind of policy which reduces the chances of your having to collect on a loved one's life insurance.

Blaze orange won't reduce the chances of a heart attack, but there are other things that will. Daily hikes for the previous couple of weeks certainly help. Heart specialist Dr. Paul Dudley White said recently that leg exercise was one of the best means of preventing heart attacks.

Have you ever noticed that many of the heart attacks occur after the hunter has shot his deer? He may die happy, but that's a poor substitute for living. We have no way of knowing, but I would guess that many of the other hunters who suffer heart attacks are lost in the woods. Probably the greatest thing to fear when you get lost is a heart attack because there isn't much else to be afraid of.

Whether you shoot a deer or get lost, it is an interesting experience, so sit down, relax and think about it for awhile. You'll live longer.

In addition to his blaze-orange cap and vest, the best life insurance a hunter can take into the woods is a couple of candy bars, waterproof match box, knife and, most important of all, a compass and map.

After you have shot your deer, sat and gloated over it for a half hour and dressed it out, common sense may tell you that it would be foolhardy to try to drag it out alone. However, you won't leave it for fear you will never find it again. You don't have to worry about this if you have your compass and map.

Tie your red handkerchief on a bush in an opening. Choose the road you want to head for. Travel in a straight line and pace the distance. In pacing, count every time your right foot hits the ground and say every tenth number out loud to prevent losing track.

With a simple hand compass, the forester experienced in its use can travel many miles with very little error. You can do almost as well if you hold the compass at waist level directly in front of you. Turn your body, not the compass, so when the needle settles you are facing the direction you wish to go. Now draw an imaginary line across it with your eye. Raise your head, following the imaginary line, until you pick some object in the distance. Walk straight toward it, but as soon as possible choose another object on the line beyond it. This keeps you going in a sraight line. When you reach the road, mark the spot and record your paces. After finding your deer-dragging partner, both you and he will probably be surprised at how accurately you can get back to your deer.

This system will probably work fairly well the first time you try it, but a little practice during the next two weeks, while you are taking your conditioning walks, is highly recommended. You will soon learn to change direction in order to circumvent swamps and other obstacles.

Don't buy too cheap a compass. It may work as well, but if it cost 98 cents you won't trust it. Any compass will show general direction, but some will do more. One of the latter is the Silva—either Type 5 at $2.50 or Type 3 (liquid filled) at $4.95. One reason for recommending these is the excellent instructions that are supplied with them.

Last Sunday, using my Type 3 Silva according to instructions, I hiked directly in to three potholes shown on an aerial photo. Ducks were there, too, and I won't blame the compass for what followed.

This compass works well at night, too, but it is much better to spend a night in the woods than to overwork trying to get out. Deer hunting can be as safe as it is enjoyable. Just remember that you went hunting to relax and you want to be around to hunt next year.

Wildlife—A Product of the Land

Spring is the courting season. The quacking hen mallard leads a pair of drake suitors through a course of aerial maneuvers. The scaup drake swims before his lady fair, puffing out his breast and stretching his neck over his back. The gaudy cock pheasant on the hillside beats his wings and crows, proclaiming domain over his territory and all the drab hens he can retain within it. And the ruffed grouse struts his log and drums.

This is the time, too, that hunters strive to calculate game abundance and prognosticate success of their beloved fall sport.

But such calculations are quite impossible because two-thirds of the pheasants and grouse and over half of the ducks to be sought by hunters next fall have yet to pip the shells of their eggs. It is the success of hatching and rearing which largely determines the abundance of game to be.

It is the hunter more than anyone else who is willing to spend his energy and his money throughout the year for the game he wants to match wits with in the fall. Unfortunately, when game becomes less abundant, he sometimes jumps to conclusions which may be more obvious than accurate. When populations of pheasants, ducks or grouse decline, the blame is often placed on foxes, skunks, or excessive hunting. The hunter wants action, too, and he is willing to pay for it. He is ready to invest in more and bigger refuges, predator control, larger contributions to Ducks Unlimited and possibly even in game farms for artificial reproduction.

This is as it has been for a long time, but sportsmen are becoming more sophisticated, a bit less vocal and a bit more analytical. Many are taking the long view, trying to see the big picture and to ferret out the

Cock and Hen Pheasant

fundamental change which could be responsible for a reduction in game abundance.

Doing this, they soon realize that the numbers of various species of predators fluctuate widely year to year and that game populations do not rise and fall in inverse proportion. They see some increase in hunting, but a little study convinces them that this could not account for a pheasant or ruffed grouse decline though it may influence waterfowl populations.

Eventually they reach the conclusion that one thing which has really changed is the environment, the place where wildlife must live and raise its young.

This is a slow and insidious change, not nearly as easily recognized as an abrupt rise or fall in the numbers of foxes or skunks. But it is a constant change, a seemingly irreversible change. Each year a few more marshes are drained, a few more sloughs are filled and, as little farms are

Hen pheasant "icing up" in a blizzard, about to die but revived when put in my car trunk. Illustrates deficient winter cover.

combined to make big ones, fence rows, woodlots and little uncultivated patches disappear.

To replace this loss of habitat, the sportsmen struggle valiantly to save wetlands and expand refuges and wildlife management areas. This is all to the good. Every bit helps, but the sportsman and the professional conservationist alike must sit back and figure the percentages.

Ninety-eight percent of the ducks on this continent are raised not on refuges, public wetlands or waterfowl production projects, but on privately owned land. Private individuals own three-fourths of Minnesota's 51-million acres and 99 percent of the land in the prime pheasant range is in private ownership.

So let's forget deer and ruffed grouse for the moment and figure the percentages on ducks and pheasants. As important as our refuges and waterfowl management areas are, should all our effort be devoted to the

Ducks on a South Dakota marsh

land which produces only two percent of our ducks? And should all the money be spent on one percent of the land in the pheasant range? It seems safe to conclude that if every acre of publicly owned land were producing ducks and pheasants to capacity, these lands alone could not produce enough game for a one-day hunting season.

The hunter who figures the percentages soon realizes that he is indebted to the man on the land for producing the game he hunts and that he has an obligation to assist the landowner in continuing to produce this wildlife. The landowner, too, has an obligation, not to the hunter perhaps, but a moral obligation to himself, to all mankind and to the land over which he has temporary domain. It is an obligation to maintain some of the natural beauty and the wildlife inherent to his little piece of earth.

But the obligation to perpetuate natural beauty and wildlife is not confined to the hunter and the farmer. Every citizen and every taxpayer of this nation should be willing to contribute something toward keeping America beautiful.

A bare farm with every square foot raising corn and beans may yield the most dollars, but it is ugly to look at. It produces little wildlife and is a barren place to live.

A pond, a marsh, a wooded grove, a winding creek with trees along its banks and a little patch of wildlife food make a farm a thing of beauty, a place where wildlife thrives and a lovely setting for a home where growing children can find exciting things to do and where they will develop a love of earth.

America's affluent society can afford such beauty and it is now possible, through farm programs, for the farmer, the sportsman and the taxpayer to each contribute a little in order to maintain and increase the environment of beauty which is the home of wildlife.

The man on the land who wants this environment will find substantial cost-sharing and technical assistance through the Agricultural Stabilization and Conservation Service (ASCS) and the Soil Conservation Service (SCS). This is the taxpayer's contribution.

Now, in most states, there is a new program which makes the sportsmen's money available to the farmer for these purposes. Recently announced by the Minnesota Division of Game and Fish, this program makes state game and fish money available for technical, financial and material assistance in improving land for wildlife.

Neither the federal nor the state programs obligate the farmer in any way to permit hunting on his land. It is his land and he controls it. But up to 90 percent of the cost of making a farm beautiful and productive of wild things is available through federal and state funds.

Economic trends have not been kind to farmers in the past few decades. Only the most shrewd and sagacious businessmen have been able to survive on the farm. But many have succeeded and their farms are large.

We can only hope that they see their farms as something more than factories. Those who choose to bring beauty and wildlife back to America should be assisted ungrudgingly by the taxpayer and the sportsman. The job cannot be done on the limited land in public ownership.

Doves—Game or Songbirds?

Two subjects I have never written about are fish spearing and dove hunting. To claim that the neglect of these emotion-ridden topics was merely coincidence would be something less than the truth. It is difficult to write anything about either of these subjects without making approximately 50% of the readers mad at you. So, to avoid them is merely a matter of being politic or—is it downright cowardly?

Let's try the subject of dove hunting. In an issue of the magazine, *National Wildlife,* the editor gave equal space to two authors. One was the president of a state dove-protective association and the other a wildlife photographer and hunter. This, too, might be considered either a politic or a cowardly way of covering a subject.

The thing that makes this debate such a "sticky" one is that nearly all of the biological facts support the views of the hunter, but the sentiment, and there is nothing wrong with sentiment, is all on the side of the dove protector.

Throughout central and southern states, mourning doves are a major game bird. Some twenty million of them are shot each year. In fact, more doves are killed with shotguns than all the ducks and geese combined. According to federal law, the dove is a migratory game bird and, in recent years, the killing of more and more of them has been permitted under federal regulations. In spite of this, the continental dove population continues to increase. In 1963, North Dakota had their first dove season and the following year they estimated an increase of about one-third in the dove population. In the face of apparently heavy kills, the gun takes only about 10% of the dove population. This appears to be well within the allowable harvestable surplus, so doves continue to prosper.

In spite of the fact that they lay only two eggs, they seem to have a high rate of reproduction because doves will nest up to twelve times in a single year.

Southern hunters are very happy about the fact that many of the northern states don't hunt doves, but northern hunters scream that they are being robbed of the birds which are raised in their own back yards.

The fact they are raised in back yards, and front yards, too, is the very reason that hunters in northern states are not permitted to shoot them and perhaps never will be. The dove's greatest defense is his plaintive, mournful coo, friendliness toward man, graceful flight on whistling wings, and the fact that he is a bird of the Bible and the symbol of peace with an olive branch in his bill.

It is no doubt true that a September hunting season for mourning doves would have no effect on the following year's population. It might mean that a few less were shot in southern states or that not so many died from other causes, but the chances that a pair would again nest in your yard would probably remain unchanged.

Can you explain these cold and ruthless statistics to Mom and the three kids who have watched a pair of mourning doves build a crude stick nest outside the window, seen the eggs laid and watched the young grow amazingly fast as the loving parents pump "dove milk," digested food from their own stomachs, down the throats of the babies?

Try it some day just as Mom and the kids are watching the fledglings about to leave the nest, ready to soar into the sky on sure, swift wings and to explore the wild world they were born in. That's when you should try explaining to Mom and the kids that it doesn't make any difference if Dad goes out and blasts at these beautiful, lovable birds with his 12-gauge shotgun.

Shooting mourning doves out of trees or off of telephone wires is not sporting and we presume a law could be passed which would prohibit it. This is not what the sportsman wants. When hunted over watering areas or feed grounds, the mourning dove is an illusive target and a real challenge to the gunner. Sportsmen claim that where dove hunting is permitted it provides millions of hours of good wholesome outdoor recreation. Northern sportsmen also contend that it would be wonderful to have a game bird season in September when all other seasons are closed. This would provide an incentive to get people out-of-doors during one of the most beautiful months of the year. It would stimulate travel and bolster the economy at a time when resort business is falling off.

But the cool logic of these arguments will make no impression on the large fraternity of dove protectors. They love doves, and to protect something they love from being shot is all the logic they need or want. And the fact that the dove protector may be eating lamb chops from a Biblical animal and wearing a pheasant feather hat from a bird far more beautiful than the dove will have no bearing on the debate.

Should the sentimental arguments of the dove protectors be ruled out because they ignore reason? Of course not. This world would be just as barren without sentiment as it would be if man were devoid of logic.

So what did this article accomplish? I'll tell you before it happens. My nonhunting, bird-loving friends will say, "You didn't have to present all the facts in favor of the opposition." And my hunting friends will say, "You didn't have to get so all-fired sentimental about those doves." This may prove that discussing a sentiment-ridden controversial subject makes not 50%, but 100% of the readers mad at you.

Memory of a Cooper's Hawk

It wasn't a particularly good place to see a deer, but the view was excellent and the log so comfortable to sit on that I stayed quite awhile. From the edge of the lowland black ash forest behind me I could see out over a large area of marsh grass. A smart deer wouldn't be caught out there during the second day of the hunting season, but there was always the hope that one might be driven across. If so, this would offer one of the rare opportunities to best use a scope-sighted 30-06 rifle in Minnesota.

Just as I had decided to be a little more serious about my hunting and move on, a Cooper's hawk darted out of the woods behind me and flew a quarter mile to the other side of the opening. These are beautiful birds, about the size of a crow, with sleek bullet-shaped bodies, long tails and short, rounded wings. They remind one of an aerial combat plane which, in fact, they are. Seldom seen circling high in the sky, these are truly woods hawks. Normally they do not fly fast, but when in pursuit of prey they have tremendous speed and can dart through the forest like a ruffed grouse. Usually they are bird hunters and frequently earn the name of "chicken hawk."

However, like all predators, they take that species of prey which is most abundant and thus play their essential part in balancing nature's wheel. Those species which are relatively scarce are not sought, while the concentrated hunt goes on for bird or mammal which has become plentiful.

As the hawk reached the woods on the other side of the opening, he made a loud cackling noise which has best been described by E. H. Forbush who wrote, "When the Cooper's loud 'clucks' ring through the sunny, leafy woods of June, the hush of death pervades everything. All erstwhile, cheerful thrushes and warblers become still and silent. The Cooper's fierce clucks are the most merciless sounds of our summer woods. There is indeed death in the air."

The hawk darted along the edge of the woods until he met another of his kind. They rose straight up in aerial combat, and the chattering noise which they made sounded as if it were coming from many birds. The battle was brief. The vanquished departed and the victor took his place on a high snag to wait and watch.

I have heard that no hill is large enough for two lions and no home big enough for two women. It would appear that no hunting territory is large enough for two Cooper's hawks. Can it be that these hawks are as cantankerous as lions?

As I watched, the hawk dove quickly from his treetop perch into the tall grass below. In moments he was back on his perch again holding a small rodent in his talons. The first course of his breakfast menu was quickly eaten. Then he moved on to another snag to watch. At this time and place apparently mice, not birds, were most abundant. As I watched, it became obvious that this bird was a far better hunter than I. My high-powered rifle was no match for his skill and equipment. His eyes can recognize an object many times out of range of the human eye. My bullet may travel a little faster than he can but it does not have the deadly accuracy and it cannot swerve around a tree. But then, I don't have his incentive to hunt either. He must be a skillful hunter or starve, and considering the fact that he must be a successful hunter every day during every season of the year, I do not begrudge his superior hunting equipment. My stomach is very glad that it need not depend on my hunting skill to keep it filled.

Now the hawk was gone, the show was over. I had had my hunting lesson for the day and decided to put it to practice. Back in the black ash woods I located a deer trail and right beside it was a stump completely covered with soft green moss. The velvet-covered stool looked so inviting that I sat. It was so comfortable that I stayed sitting until a fine big buck came slowly ambling down the trail. As he walked among the large ash trees only parts of him were now and then exposed—always the wrong parts. At last a front leg and front shoulder appeared in the scope. The aim was good, the bullet true, and the hunt was over. The hunting was over but the work began.

Author and his buck

Unwilling to admit that I am not as strong and able to drag a deer as in my youth, it must be that Minnesota is growing bigger deer these days. It is at times like this that one really appreciates his hunting partner even though said partner gripes continuously during the dragging-out ordeal.

Within a few years this hunt will be forgotten or at least indistinguishably jumbled up with other enjoyable hunts. The hunting demonstration by the Cooper's hawk will remain much longer in my memory.

The Ethics of Duck Hunting

There is nothing like duck hunting to make a man humble. I was out alone this morning and quickly made two clean kills on fine mallards with the first two shells. Betsy, my over and under Browning double, and I were alternately congratulating each other on exceptional skill, fine workmanship, proper lead, excellent balance and good teamwork.

Another pair of mallards came over and Betsy insisted that with her help I could make a clean double and go home with my limit of four ducks, having fired only four shells. She knew as well as I that the limit of mallards was two, but it took all of my power of persuasion plus my respect for the law to permit the mallards to pass.

Then a flock of some twenty mallards circled and hovered almost motionless over the decoys before moving on. Betsy proffered the idea that she should have her limit of two mallards as well as I. She wouldn't settle down until I asked her to show me her license and duck stamp. She didn't take kindly to this, but I assured her that before long a couple of bluebills would come by and we would conclude the day's hunt strictly within the law.

Finally a flock of bluebills did circle the lake several times, teasing us by swinging just out of range. At last they decided to visit our decoys and, as they came at a slight angle, I threw Betsy to my shoulder and assured her that she had but to bark twice more and the hunt would be over.

Then the 'bills headed straight for us, and the one I had pulled on suddenly looked smaller and farther away. During the instant when I should have been squeezing Betsy's trigger on the first duck and having

Mallards

the rest flare up in easy range in front of me, I made the mistake of wait-ing for them to get closer. Suddenly they flared up over my head and all I could find to point at was blue sky in which, in desperation, I shot a hole.

Did I apologize to Betsy? Of course not. That would not be within the true tradition of duck hunting. Among the duck hunting fraternity, apologies and admissions of poor marksmanship are inexcusable. Under these circumstances, one must alibi, make excuses and exaggerate.

There are several approved methods of doing this, and the poorer one shoots, the larger must be his repertoire of alibis. It is quite ethical to accuse your partner or dog of rocking the boat at the moment you were squeezing the trigger. Most frequently used is the alibi which calls for a certain amount of pantomime as well as well-chosen words.

After missing with both barrels, the hunter slowly lowers his gun and, with parted lips, watches in utter amazement as the supposedly dead duck flies on. Then, deliberately, he states, "That duck is loaded with shot. Watch him. He's sure to drop out there somewhere." One of my favorites is, "Out of range, of course. But then I like to hear the gun fire."

Other acceptable excuses include: "Did you hear the pellets hit that fellow? These northerns really have heavy feathers." "This number six shot I'm using is just too fine for these big, high-flying ducks." "With this number four shot, my gun throws a lousy pattern. That duck flew right through it."

But while excuses, alibis and exaggerations are all an accepted part of duck hunting, certain illegal and, more important, unethical acts are strictly taboo.

Once this fall, while hunting with a companion, a pair of young hunters nearby were doing a great deal of shooting with phenomenally poor success. Then, to our amazement, one of them rowed out and picked up two of the ducks which we had shot. Also lying in front of us was a third duck, mortally wounded and unable either to swim or fly. The invad-ing young hunter shot it, rowed over and picked it up.

"Are you sure that's your duck?" I called.

"Of course I'm sure," he replied. "I just shot him."

Legally he was quite right, but the unfortunate lad was oblivious of the true joys of duck hunting.

Canada goose protecting nest

At the turn of the century, President Grover Cleveland wrote in the ponderous style of his time, "In the estimation of many people, all those who for any purpose or in any manner hunt ducks are grouped together and indiscriminately called duck hunters. This is a very superficial way of dealing with an important subject."

One violation that offends me more than any other is shooting ahead of the permissible time. It is even more unethical than it is illegal. The "sooner" robs law-abiding hunters of the best shoot of the day which nearly always comes during the first few minutes.

On the opening day this year the shooting was to begin at noon. It was clear and calm. You could hear voices all around the bay. Suddenly, fifteen minutes early, two shots were fired and a young voice shouted, "I got him! I got him!"

In my loudest voice I added, "And it could cost you fifty bucks!"

Not another shot was fired on our bay until exactly 12 o'clock.

Though my old game and fish director badge with the number one on it is little more than a souvenir now, I would not hesitate, having proper evidence and witnesses, to make a citizen's arrest.

In these days of too few ducks, too many hunters and low limits, the number of ducks one is likely to shoot does not warrant all of the equipment and energy required in duck hunting. But wildfowling is an old and venerable sport, bound in tradition, ethics and sportsmanship.

A recent national survey shows that the number of fishermen in this nation is increasing faster than population growth, but the number of hunters is on the decline. I believe this is due less to a shortage of game than to abandonment of the principles, ethics and traditions which have been associated throughout the world with high-quality hunting. The sporting ethics still faithfully adhered to in old countries are falling apart in America—and the hunter is losing the substance of his sport.

Rowdies on the duck marsh who shoot early, steal ducks and blast at every high-flying flock before it has a chance to settle in destroy the spirit of wildfowling. But how do we teach and instill good manners and ethics which are the basis of sportsmanship and quality hunting?

Waterfowl Regulations

Of twenty million hunters in the United States, only about two million hunt waterfowl. But there are no more ardent hunters than those whose favorite sport is matching wits with ducks and geese in the fall.

It is an expensive sport compared to most hunting. A waterfowl hunter not only spends an additional $3 for a duck stamp, but buys much specialized equipment such as duck boats, trailers, decoys, calls and special clothes. He may also invest heavily in leasing or buying a place to hunt, traveling long distances for better hunting and, more than any other sportsman, he contributes to organizations dedicated to preserving waterfowl habitat.

Because he invests much in his sport and even more because the most pleasant and memorable of all his hours are spent in a duck blind, the waterfowl hunter is the most vociferous of all hunters about season lengths and bag limits.

It is well known to all conservation administrators that hunters in general tend to demand seasons which over-restrict hunting on resident game such as deer, pheasants and grouse, but insist on liberal seasons which may overharvest the migratory birds. This attitude appears to stem from a desire to build or stockpile nonmigratory birds so there will be better hunting next year. On the other hand, hunters of each state insist on getting their share and perhaps a bit more of the birds which migrate through and may be shot elsewhere.

The fact is you cannot stockpile any species above the carrying capacity of its range, and excessive hunting can reduce a wildlife population below that carrying capacity. Thus, while we usually underharvest our resident game, wasting that which exceeds the carrying capacity, we are constantly on the verge of overharvesting ducks which are shot at for four months or more in their southward migration from Canada to the wintering grounds which may be in Mexico.

Predictions of the number of ducks that would be flying south the fall of 1968 were anything but encouraging. Traditionally, predictions of the fall flight by the U. S. Fish and Wildlife Service are conservative while those of Ducks Unlimited are optimistic. That year even Ducks Unlimited predictions contained nothing to gladden the hearts of duck hunters.

Apparently the northward flight of breeding ducks in the spring was satisfactory. But the surveys strongly indicate that breeding success was well below par and, in the average year, duck hunters harvest more young than adult ducks. Why breeding success was poor during a summer of apparently heavy rainfall which should have kept the potholes full is not easily understood by duck hunters.

I am not sure the professionals fully understand it either, but there seems to be one reason which would at least partially explain the failure of breeding ducks to bring off abundant large broods.

Snow was relatively light that winter and early spring was very dry. Migrating ducks, moving north as quickly as the ice melted, found dry potholes and marshes in their favorite breeding grounds in the Dakotas, western Minnesota and the southern portion of the prairie provinces of Canada. So they continued to fly north until they found water.

The reason is not fully understood, but when ducks can nest in the Dakotas and the southern provinces, production is usually high. When they are forced to fly farther north, it is low.

Duck hunters are understandably disappointed to hear the gloomy reports which result in further restrictions of their favorite sport. Some hunters, on the basis of their own observations, refuse to believe the predicted decline and have written me letters requesting that I refute this "nonsense" and pay attention to the "old-time hunters and guides."

They must have forgotten that as Minnesota's State Director of Game and Fish I constantly worked for longer, more realistic seasons on deer and other resident game but, at flyway council meetings, I always represented the conservative element because I believed our harvest of ducks was maximum if not excessive.

It is perfectly natural that hunters make their own predictions of game abundance by what they see in their own localities. These predictions may be reasonably accurate in the case of local nonmigratory game. But the ducks and broods I see in the few lakes and potholes familiar to me is no basis for predicting duck numbers on the North American continent or even in our Mississippi Flyway.

Between 1935 and 1947 the U. S. Fish and Wildlife Survey based waterfowl regulations on a winter count of ducks made in early January. This proved to be grossly unreliable for two reasons. Winter counts are never very accurate, and they do not take into account the breeding season which produces most of the ducks the hunters take.

For the past twenty years, waterfowl estimates have been based largely upon aerial surveys of the breeding grounds which are flown in May and again in July. Flying at an altitude of 100 feet over the same designated routes each year, two-man teams of a pilot-biologist and an observer record the water areas and the breeding waterfowl they see for a distance of 220 yards on each side of the plane during the May survey.

The same aerial transects are again flown in July to measure the reproductive success of the breeding ducks. These aerial transects range from seven to twenty miles apart in areas which produce many ducks and up to sixty miles apart in the scattered breeding grounds of the far north. Ducks Unlimited also conduct surveys, and there are special study areas to determine the rate of reproduction. Even with this large sample the error may be up to 20 percent.

Unfortunately, the production survey must be completed well before the end of July because the law requires that hunting regulations be established and published in the Federal Register thirty days before the opening of the earliest waterfowl hunting season. If this survey could be delayed a few weeks, estimates of waterfowl production success would be much more accurate.

Pressures, political and otherwise, are brought to bear in establishing waterfowl seasons and bag limits. Nearly always these pressures demand more liberal duck-hunting regulations. Such pressures cannot be totally ignored by the director of the U. S. Fish and Wildlife Service or the Secretary of the Interior.

When a powerful congressman with little regard for the resource threatens budget cuts or the elimination of conservation programs if his hunting constituents are not taken care of, the Secretary has a difficult decision. But usually the Secretary gives first consideration to the resource and accepts the recommendations of his professional staff. May it always be thus.

Grouse Hunting With Zeke

If success is measured by meat in the bag, the first two days of grouse hunting seemed to be generally poor. But, if measured by pleasant hours afield, it should have rated not poor but rich.

It was a warm, sunny weekend and, because of abundant late-summer rains, the woods were soft, quiet and green, with dashes of yellow and orange of the ash, birch and poplar leaves with a few maples turning red and the scarlet sumac leaves dropping from the branches.

Asked if the hunters were getting many birds, a country storekeeper replied, "No, and some of them are convinced there just aren't any partridge in the woods. But in a few weeks they may wonder where they all came from."

The ruffed grouse (partridge) may or may not be plentiful this year. It is too soon to tell. But they were not concentrated along the roads and trails where hunters usually find them.

This is the first year I have used my black Lab Zeke for partridge hunting, and he obviously agrees with me that it is a fine form of recreation even though he had an experience which might well have discouraged a dog of lesser stature.

Ambling down a woods trail, he paid little heed to my suggestion that he enjoy the abundance of beautiful mushrooms and various types of shell fungus along with all the greenery which is absent in dry falls. He didn't even seem to appreciate the purple asters and the red berries of the little false lilies of the valley. But perhaps his sensitive nose made him aware of many woodsy things that I was missing. At any rate, Zeke was highly exuberant about the whole trip.

Ruffed grouse on nest

The trail ended. I sat down to light my pipe and Zeke sat down on the trail. Suddenly Zeke jumped up and dashed into the woods behind me. Thinking he had surely spotted or smelled a grouse, I dropped my pipe and grabbed my shotgun. A second look at Zeke told me that he was a dog running, not toward something, but away from something. I looked back to where he had been sitting and saw a hole in the ground with bees funneling out of it like a column of smoke. Well, they were either bees or yellowjackets or hornets or something. Curiosity did not stay my hasty retreat.

I have hunted with many breeds of dogs, including setters, but that was the first day I had ever hunted with a sitter. One of the bees had assaulted Zeke dead center under his tail, and his progress thereafter was interrupted by frequent sits and little slides. It probably was much less funny to him than to me, but when I laughed he seemed to enjoy the joke along with me. I am convinced that many dogs have a sense of humor and can even enjoy a joke on themselves.

There are two ways to shoot grouse. You can shoot them as they sit on the ground along the side of a road or trail or you can flush them and take your chances on a wing shot as they dart among the trees and bushes at remarkable speed.

Probably 80 percent of all grouse shot are stationary targets, and there is nothing more ridiculous than to ask your hunting partner or your dad when he comes home from the hunt whether he shot his bird sitting or flying. According to him they were all tough wing shots and you never believe a word of it. You probably won't even believe me when I insist that I would never shoot such a sporty target without giving it a chance to fly.

The hunter who hikes the trails and trailless woods with an active dog has a good deal more shooting than one who drives the roads watching the ditches. But, before the leaves fall, he may not bring home as much meat.

Grouse hunting can be a leisurely, ambling sort of sport. But if you are going to shoot these little woods darters on the wing it also requires more readiness and alertness than any sport I know—particularly before the leaves have fallen. You don't throw your gun over your shoulder or dangle it in one hand.

You walk holding it with both hands. At the first sound of rapidly beating wings, the gun starts up and the safety is pushed off before you see anything. There is no time for the carefully planned swing and lead. It is snap shooting at its best, and grouse hunters put a lot more lead into tree trunks than they do into grouse.

Ruffed grouse are most unpredictable birds. They can be extremely wary or totally unafraid. I once stood six feet from one sitting on a low branch and kicked dirt at it in a vain effort to make it fly. Finally it jumped off the limb and walked away into a spruce bog, the smarter for having been dumb.

Now that I have explained in detail the art of grouse shooting and how to go about it, you must realize that I am one of the most competent of grouse hunters—well qualified to instruct the experienced as well as the neophytes.

Of course, there was that embarrassing incident last fall when a partner and I hunted far and wide from sunrise to dark and returned with nothing more edible than excuses. As we walked into our cabin we smelled grouse cooking. Mrs. K. had walked a quarter of a mile down the trail and knocked off a couple for dinner.

Let me see now, is there anything I have forgotten to mention about my hunt on this fall's opening weekend? Oh, yes, I didn't tell you how many grouse I shot. Well, let's consider that an "oversight," or was it an "underlead"?

PART II

ESKIMO LAND

Eskimo boy—happy as usual.

Arctic Alaska

To consider this a complete account of Alaska would be unfair to our 49th state. It is not a story of the lovely forested, snowcapped mountains, inland waterways, luxurious hotels, boat rides in the harbors and ferry trips among the islands. Seacoasts warmed by the Japanese Current and the land of the big strawberries are not a part of this tale.

We hope this story will paint a picture of the vast, sparsely settled new portion of this nation from Nome north which is Arctic Alaska. This is the treeless land of bush pilots, Eskimos and empty oil barrels—of driftwood, days without light and nights without darkness.

Beauty, as we have learned it, is missing from the Arctic. Superficially it is ugly. But, those who search the Arctic's soul find beauty of an unexpected kind in the strong character of its foreboding countenance. It is a beauty not akin to the soft skin and supple form of feminine youth but to the strength and character of furrowed face and gnarled knuckles of a man of the sea.

The Arctic is unbelievably vast, barren and harsh. Its summer smile is brief and tenuous. Its buried bounty of gold, oil and copper is yielded reluctantly from permanently frozen earth and rocks. Fresh water is available only from melted snow. It is a cruel land, relentless and unforgiving. It disdains the soft, gentle, weak and incompetent.

The Arctic is a land of snow, ice, wind and frozen seas. It invites or welcomes none. It tolerates only the strong. Begrudgingly it permits the existence, but constantly tests the strength, of the polar bear, walrus and Eskimo.

149

The route we traveled.

Men go to the Arctic hoping to gain fortune and to return. Most return, with or without fortune, but a few are captured by the excitement, ceaseless challenge and the inward reward of mastery of the elements.

I had a taste of the excitement when three bull walrus attacked our vulnerable boat of driftwood and walrus skin; when trying to catch birds in a tiny net on the end of a 14-foot pole; and when scaling the rocks to see and photograph auklets, puffins and murres. The reward of achievement was experienced while standing on the one spot on earth where it is possible to see two oceans, two continents, two days and the two major world powers.

Endeavoring to understand the Eskimo was the greatest challenge. Entering his home through a tunnel in the rocks and a hole in the floor is strange, but it can be explained by the Eskimo's physical relationship with the elements. But roots of the vanishing Eskimo culture run deep into soils of survival, superstition and skill.

Good fortune more than good planning blessed me with a memorable taste of Arctic Alaska. I hope my diary and camera have made it possible for you to share this experience.

*   *   *   *

NOME, ALASKA

When I was a naughty child my mother would say, "I'm going to pack you off to Nome, Alaska!" Then, as now, it seemed to me that Nome was the end of the earth and I never thought I could be really bad enough to get there. But here I am.

Though it seems that we have been here a week, it was just this morning that Dr. Walter J. (Breck) Breckenridge, director of the University of Minnesota Museum of Natural History, and I arrived here by plane from Anchorage.

Breck is here to study birds, to take more pictures for his forthcoming movie on bird migration and to exercise his considerable talent as a wildlife artist. I, too, am interested in the birds which come to the Arctic to build their homes and raise their young, but perhaps I am even more eager to learn about the people and places of this young state.

More than anything, I want to get acquainted with the Eskimos, to learn how they live and what they think. How the white man is influencing their way of life seems important, but most of all I hope to find remote villages where the ancient Eskimo culture still prevails.

I also hope to learn the probable fate of some of the great Arctic animals such as the walrus and polar bear, the effect that netting has on island nesting birds and, I hope, something about that strange little animal, the lemming, whose numbers rise and fall in the greatest of all animal cycles. I should like to learn if it is really true that they make great death marches to the sea.

The conundrum about Nome is why it is here at all. You wonder how anyone can make a living and, at the same time, looking at the muddy dirt roads and the tacky, shacky homes, you wonder if anyone really does make a living—at least anyone not working for the state or federal governments.

Kayak Frame

What supports the place? With no agriculture, industry, harbor or other visible means of support, it sits on the coast of the Arctic Sea behind a great rubble wall of giant rocks built by the United States army engineers to keep high seas from washing it away.

Nome was born with the big gold strike which came in 1898 when three fabulous Swedes started the gold mine which became known as the million-dollars-a-week mine. By 1900 Nome had a population of 30,000, including 400 lawyers.

The present population of Nome is less than a tenth that of the gold rush days and about 70% of the inhabitants are Eskimos.

In 1901, two men, fighting over a "madam," kicked over a lantern and seven square blocks of the town went up in smoke. That was the first of several disastrous fires.

There is still gold around Nome, but the high-grade ore is gone. A few still mine, but the second largest gold dredge in the world sits on the edge of town, its owners hoping the price of gold will be raised.

The beach at Nome

Nome is both the ugliest and the most interesting town you could find. It is largely a city of shacks sitting on heavy wooden beams which lie on the ground. Clothes hang from lines and Tom Cod hang drying from horizontal poles at rooftops. Streets are muddy or dusty, and it is thirty miles to the nearest tree.

Permafrost, which means the ground is perpetually frozen, is a major problem. Buildings cannot have basements or even foundations. When heaving ground puts houses so out of kilter that doors no longer swing, the beams which support them are jacked and shimmed until the floor becomes temporarily more level.

The new school building has a refrigeration system keeping the ground under it from thawing in summer to prevent shifting and cracking.

To obtain water or dispose of sewage in frozen ground is no small problem. There are no outhouses in the Arctic. All wastes must be carried to the sea. Under some streets utilidors are being built. These are tunnels, four feet wide and six feet high, made of three-inch thick planks. Through these, water and sewer pipes will run.

Umiak with new walrus-hide cover.

That there are only 250 miles of road which can be reached from Nome does not reduce the use of cars which must be brought in by boat or plane. The 600 cars represent better than one per family.

Of the 200,000 plus inhabitants of Alaska, 10,000 are Indians and 30,000 are Eskimos. The Eskimos are increasing far more rapidly than the whites and Nome proves it.

Eskimo kids are everywhere and their bright red and blue parkas and jackets give Nome its only touch of color.

I like these kids. They are self-sufficient, polite, friendly and cute as the dickens. A few shy little girls duck when you aim your camera, but most of them beam at you in delight.

On the east end of Nome live the King Islanders—a group of Eskimos who long survived on tiny precipitous King Island some 50 miles out in the Arctic Ocean. Most of them moved to Nome where, by comparison, living is easy. However, some move back to their island in the fall to spend the winters in their tiny shacks clinging to the mountainsides along the sea.

This is the seal and walrus hunting season and the King Island Eskimos take to the sea in their oomiaks. In winter they range over the miles of shore ice by dog team and hunt seal in the floating ice from tiny kayaks.

The oomiak is a remarkable boat which is used on the open sea. It is 25 to 35 feet long and over 6 feet wide. For generations they were propelled only by paddles and sails, but Eskimos, being naturally good mechanics, were quick to accept the outboard motor.

The oomiak, or "skin boat," frame is diligently made of wood—whatever kind of wood drifts in to shore. It is covered with the outer layer of split walrus hide which could easily be mistaken for fiber glass and is even tougher. This might seem a primitive-type boat to be still in use on the open seas, but when you see them it is hard to conceive how it could be improved upon. They are very light, tough and of excellent design. They are slid over the shore ice for miles to reach open water with no damage, and dragging them up on stony beaches doesn't mar the tough walrus hide.

The most precise art in building oomiaks, which is known only to a few Eskimo women, is splitting the walrus hides to exactly the right thickness and sewing the pieces together in a unique waterproof fold.

When properly shaped, the skin blanket is stretched, wet and soft, over the frame. It dries like the head of a drum.

Before leaving Nome we watched the first ship of the year arrive. To say it arrived means it came within half a mile and dropped anchor where it waited for tugboats towing barges to come and gather their purchased loot.

It had been eight months since the last ship came to Nome and store supplies had become progressively more scare and expensive. Three ships come to Nome each year—in June, July and October.

Nome becomes more interesting each day and we hope there will be another opportunity to feel the pulse of this village. But tomorrow we take a "bush" flight to the Eskimo village of Wales on the western tip of the Seward Peninsula.

Breck looks at stretched ribbon seal. (Wales)

Wales, Alaska

At last I have experienced it briefly—the life of a celebrity. How often does one see from the window of his plane the entire population of a town waiting along the runway to greet him? Where else would you have a dozen or more redcaps carrying your luggage to your Edgewater Beach Hotel? Of course, there were a few extenuating circumstances.

The village of Wales, Alaska lies on the western tip of the Seward Peninsula. It is a little south of the Arctic Circle and only thirty miles east of the Iron Curtain and a little farther from Siberia.

The population of Wales is 150 Eskimos and two whites. The redcaps were Eskimo children dressed in parkas, and our hotel was a recently vacated Eskimo house on the beach on Bering Strait. My companion, Breck (Dr. W. J. Breckenridge), had been in Wales studying and photographing birds the year before and was affectionately known as "The Birdman."

The 100-mile flight from Nome could hardly be called luxuriant, but it was interesting. Bush pilot Otis Hammonds packed Breck and me along with two passengers for other villages and 400 pounds of gear into the ancient V-77 Stinson plane and we were off.

"How old is this plane?" I shouted over the roar of the 300-horse-power motor.

With a grin Otis replied, "It was built in 1946—the first time."

I also learned that the plane had flown over 8,000 hours which, times 125 miles per hour, means a million miles.

As we approached Wales to land on the narrow strip of beach along the ice-covered sea, a crosswind swept out of the mountains and, for a

Eskimo women always work together when the game comes in. (Wales)

Mrs. Emuk, the minister's wife, getting meat for dinner. (Wales)

moment, I thought the plane might not make a million and one miles. But we zoomed up and settled in nicely on the second try.

Climbing out of the old plane on this ninth day of June, it suddenly became obvious why our greeting delegation was dressed in parkas and mukluks. The little village was locked behind a mile-wide strip of sea ice. Lingering snowdrifts were piled to the roofs of some buildings and an icy wind swept out of the mountains.

Eskimos are known as a friendly people and this they certainly are. But some say that underneath it all they neither like nor respect the white man. I have seen nothing to indicate any truth in this. They seem to like Breck and appear ready to accept me as his friend. Perhaps they judge us well as individuals rather than as a race. I hope to understand them better before our trip is over.

Having money doesn't seem to be important to the Eskimos. Their desire for it depends entirely on their immediate needs. What they will charge you for something may be entirely too high or too low. They said we could rent the house they took us to for $2 a day. This is ridiculous in this land of exorbitant prices, so, of course, we will will pay them more.

Feeling that we had just experienced the shortest summer in history, Breck and I crawled back into our long underwear, wool socks and down parkas. As we started out for the marshes and hills to study and photograph birds, we passed the home of Walter Emuk, the Eskimo minister.

Mrs. Emuk was just coming out of the house carrying two of those strange semicircular knives called ulus, or woman knives. We followed her to the snowdrift behind the house where she uncovered the hole which was filled with the gory remains of an oogruk whose bewhiskered head and flippers were still attached. The ookruk is a large seal weighing 300 pounds and considered excellent food.

On a nearby drying rack hung many pieces of oogruk which had turned black as ink. Mrs. Emuk explained that these would later be cut into thinner strips for more complete drying.

As she cut off chunks of the fresh oogruk she invited us for dinner the following evening. I had been warned by everyone who knows about Eskimo food or who has tried to eat it. They all said, "Don't—because even if you can eat it you can't keep it down."

Eskimo kids mugging at camera

Tomorrow we will know because Breck and I accepted Mrs. Emuk's dinner invitation.

As we started for the marsh we met a boy carrying a slingshot and two red phalaropes. If he doesn't get enough for a meal, they will be fed to the dogs.

Loaded with movie and still cameras, long lenses, tripods and binoculars, we set out across the marshes, meadows and mountainside which would be our observation area for several days. Breck's knowledge of natural history has been a source of amazement since my college days and it was not less inspiring here in the Arctic.

A tiny western sandpiper from Asia fluttered from the sparse ground cover. Her broken wing act told us she had left her nest. Even knowing the almost exact location of the nest, its perfect camouflage and the brown blotches on the four large eggs made it almost impossible to locate. But Breck found it and within a half hour he had made movies of the little bird settling back on her nest.

We saw, and sometimes photographed, long-billed dowitchers, golden plovers, Arctic terns, yellow wagtails, two species of phalaropes, and many more. Never did we see a bird and seldom did we hear a call which Breck could not identify.

Leaving Breck sitting motionless behind his camera, I climbed Backbone Mountain to see the Eskimo burial ground.

As I climbed, the mosses, lichens and ground-hugging plants formed a soft carpet, wet from the melting snow. A dwarf willow pushed its furry pussies an inch or two above the ground. Nothing grew taller.

Then the soft wet carpet gave way to jagged rocks turned black by the hard, black, leafy lichens which cover them.

As I reached the saddle of the mountain between two jagged rock peaks, the wind swept low clouds through the pass. It was bleak and cold.

First I saw pieces of driftwood, then very old whale ribs, guns and spears rusted to bits and many polar bear skulls. Nor were the remains of the deceased whose graves these artifacts adorned hard to find. Skeletal remains of Eskimos lay in what was left of small wooden caskets, and human skulls were scattered among the rocks.

Many skeletal remains were found beyond the pass on the side of the mountain away from the village. These were the Eskimos who had died of tuberculosis.

A raven nest clung high and inaccessible to the rocky crags above. The big black birds circled in the mist overhead, croaking and jabbering. A cold wind blew whisps of mist through the gap and all that could be seen among the black rocks were bleached bones of animals and men. It was eerie, cold and desolate, but with an atmosphere of melancholic beauty.

Far below, the little Eskimo village of Wales was outlined against the Arctic Sea. Further still were the Diomede Islands and the coast of Siberia. How many Eskimos over how many years had been carried on their last journey from the village to the mountain where I stood, not even the ravens could remember.

Back at the village, twelve-year-old Robert Tevuk, a friendly, intelligent Eskimo boy, dropped in for a visit. He told me how in summer he would go with his mother and sisters to pick berries and leaves. Blueberries and cranberries are preserved one way or another but, almost

Burial ground at Wales. This man must have been a great hunter. Note remains of gun and other hunting devices, also polar bear skulls, blue whale ribs which were carried up the mountain.

Eskimo dogs on beach. Summer is a dreary time for dogs. (Wales)

They left at midnight. (Wales)

drooling at the thought, he said, "Salmon berries and blackberries are good mixed with Eskimo ice cream."

The recipe he gave me for Eskimo ice cream is probably incomplete, but I don't expect to try it anyway. The primary ingredients are tallow, reindeer fat, seal oil and water, all beat together with snow.

Robert believes he has traveled quite a bit for a boy his age, but he has never seen a tree!

Asked whether he preferred summer or winter, Robert hesitated and then said thoughtfully, "I think summer, but not for too long. We are all very happy in August when it starts to snow."

In summer when high waves roll in from the sea, boys and girls play a game called kaiksetok. All the kids follow a receding wave as it slides back down the beach. Then they run back ahead of the next wave. If a wave catches one, he must run out and touch a wave and then beat it back to shore. "Most of us get wet," Robert said.

He also said the boys sometimes swam in the creek flowing out of the mountains and, "Once," he told me, "when it was very calm I swam in the ocean."

When I asked if he could really swim, he said, "I think if I tried real hard."

Though Eskimos extract most of their food from the sea and spend much of their time in boats or on the ice, none can swim. The water is always too cold to learn.

What are Robert's plans? He wants to go to Nome and attend high school and then come back to Wales to live. If he ever could get enough money, he would buy an airplane.

Breck and I came prepared to camp for a week near a big lagoon 10 or 20 miles north of Wales and study birds, but the sea is still frozen solid. We could get the Eskimos to take us there by dog team, but should the ice break we would have to wait until a boat could come for us and that could be well into July.

There are many birds here but they are too wild to be easily photographed. Eskimo boys, who seem to be born to hunt, are constantly pursuing them with slingshots.

The Eskimo population of Wales is far outnumbered by the dogs. By village order, all are tied. At the end of very short chains they lie among the driftwood, old oil barrels and rubble. They are not pets, but beasts of burden whose lives are spent at the end of a short chain or in harness.

These dogs seldom make much sound, but at 11 o'clock last night the pile of driftwood on the beach near us suddenly burst into frenzy. More than twenty dogs were jerking at their chains, barking, howling and wailing.

I looked out and saw two men pushing a large dog sled in their direction. Pulling the sled is the one thing these dogs live for and they were begging for harness. I went out and learned that the team was to be taken across the sea ice to bring back one of the large skin boats. The rope attached to the front of the sled seemed extremely long and I asked the owner how many he was taking.

"Thirteen," he replied. Then he smiled and said, "I have six more but won't need them for this trip."

The lead dog was first in harness and he sat quietly, keeping the line tight as the other dogs were harnessed along each side of the rope. Only the lead dog was quiet. The others howled, bayed, bit the rope and strained forward in their eagerness to be off and running.

At last the log bar driven into frozen snow to hold the sled was pulled and a command was shouted. The lead dog sprang into action and two men on a sled were sailing across the snow at the foot of a mountain. Then they turned out to sea where the white mist and white ice were as one. They looked like ghost riders in the sky as I watched them fade into the fog.

*   *   *   *

Anticipating a gastronomical experience, if not an ordeal, we arrived at the Emuk residence at 6:30 for our dinner engagement.

We had seen oogruk turned inky black hanging from the drying racks, peered into "meat holes" where walrus sometimes gets even too "high" to suit Eskimo tastes, and watched men carefully divide kokh (walrus skin and blubber). We knew that ookruk intestines were considered a delicacy, and we had seen the Eskimo women on the mountainside picking leaves which are preserved in seal oil. We also knew that

The new and the old schools—Wales.

Breck with young Eskimo audience preparing a scientific mount of a crested auklet.

traditionally Eskimos ate sitting on the floor using only their fingers and mother's ulu (woman's knife) for utensils.

With these observations in mind, we were surprised, on entering the Emuk home, to see the table, clean and neat, with tablecloth and set with knives, forks and spoons all in their proper places. We sat down with Mr. and Mrs. Emuk and the two boys. Three daughters waited on us. Our menu included mashed potatoes, fresh liver, spinach and canned fruit.

Knowing the gastronomic frailties of our race, they had proudly and most politely prepared a meal to suit our customs and our tastes. We had pleasant conversation and left happy and well fed but no better informed about the eating habits of Eskimos.

*   *   *   *

At 3 p.m. on June 11 there was a knock at the door on our Eskimo house in Wales, Alaska. I opened it and the visitor and I looked at each other with equal surprise because each had expected to see an Eskimo and neither did.

"A white man lives here!" my visitor said in a Spanish accent. He was Father Llorente, a priest who had just returned from a 49-day stay on Little Diomede Island.

The first boat of Diomede hunters had arrived from the island. The trip can be made in a little over two hours but, much to the lament of Father Llorente, it had taken over eleven hours this time. When they landed on the ice a mile away the exhausted and frustrated priest did not wait for unloading or packing, but set out immediately for Wales and went to the nearest house which happened to be the one we were in.

The story later related by the Diomede Eskimos was quite amusing to them. Father Llorente had prayed aloud that they would see no walrus along the way so that the trip would be direct and fast. This displeased the Eskimos, but only momentarily, for hardly had he uttered his prayer when walrus were sighted. Herd after herd were spotted on floating chunks of ice and the Eskimos fell to the deadly business they know and love so well.

By the time they reached Wales, after the greatest hunt of the year, they had killed 25 bulls, one cow and three calves.

Preparing to leave for Little Diomede. (Wales)

It is well known that young bull walrus will attack the boat if other walrus are wounded. Recently a boat was ripped open by their powerful tusks and the occupants survived only because they reached a large chunk of ice before the boat sank.

At one point on the trip Father Llorente, who has spent thirty years in Alaska, admitted he did a rather foolish thing. Following one of the killings, the young bulls attacked and the Father got very excited and shouted to everyone, "Shoot! Shoot!" The Eskimos just smiled because the boat had been pulled up on the ice where they all stood in perfect safety because a walrus is an awkward, almost immobile beast out of the water.

I walked out to the Diomeders' boat and worked with them getting their boat up to a safe spot and helped pack in their duffle until midnight. I'm not that nice a guy, but I was eager to get to Diomede and this was the only hope.

Breck and I had tried unsuccessfully for several days to get Wales Eskimos to take us to Diomede. We were just beginning to learn that few of them had ever been there and only the Diomeders retained the skill

The ivory tusks of 40 walrus were in umiak we took from Wales to Little Diomede.

to cross Bering Strait. Weather is seldom good and always unpredictable, and the swift complicated currents, high winds and fog of Bering Strait make navigation difficult. There is also the deadly fear of missing the little island and landing on Russian-held Big Diomede.

*   *   *   *

This day, June 12, can be recorded as one of those days which makes life more interesting and more exciting than I really had expected.

I didn't come to Alaska to hunt, but I did come to learn how these men hunt whose very existence depends upon their hunting skill.

Tommy Menadelook, captain of the boat, had agreed to take us back to Little Diomede but, of course, he didn't say when because that would depend on the weather. In this country you make plans and wait. When the weather is right you carry them out.

The fog lifted a little but the wind was still strong. Tommy poked his head in at our door and said we would go.

The old man spotted the walrus. (Bering Strait)

At 7:10 p.m. the 32-foot wood skeleton, covered with walrus hide, the oomiak, was slid off the snowbank at the edge of the mountain into the sea. Six Eskimos, Breck and I were headed for Diomede. The fog was still bad and, much to my disappointment, they decided to go directly back without hunting along the way.

One of the Eskimos, Kayouktuk, was old—not even he knows how old. Three fingers were gone from one hand. Caught in a running harpoon line, two were jerked off and the third injured. Two weeks later the third finger turned black so he took his knife out of its sheath and cut the finger off at the joint.

Kayouktuk owned the oomiak but was no longer the captain. However, he gave the orders and, out of respect for his experience, his orders were obeyed.

The temperature was about 35 degrees and a 25-mile-per-hour salt spray and fog-laden wind swept over the port side where I sat. Though wearing more clothes than any time during the winter, I was freezing. Then I learned something else about oomiaks.

At a command from the old one, they stood paddles upright along the port side and raised a canvas strip which was fastened to, and neatly

The shooting begins. (Bering Strait)

rolled along, the gunwale. The wind was gone. Comfortable now, I lit my pipe and started taking pictures of the interior of the boat.

In Nome I had admired the flowing design and fine workmanship of these skin boats built by the King Island Eskimos. They resemble the large freighter canoes which Indians built of birch bark in the voyageur days, but these have slightly more rounded bottoms and the skin is smoother than bark. Propelled by motors of 10 to 20 horsepower, they glide through the water like fish at remarkable speeds.

The boat looked ancient and I asked one man how old it was. He said, "Older than I."

"How old are you?"

"Thirty."

Every three or four years, the boats are recovered with hide from the female walrus, split to one-fourth inch thick.

Soon we were weaving among large chunks of floating ice. Breck said, "I've done many different things on Saturday nights before, but never spent one quite like this." It was the first time that either of us had actually

The young bulls ready to attack. (Bering Strait)

All they want is the two front teeth. (Bering Strait)

put to sea in a boat and here we were in a walrus-skin boat with an Eskimo captain and crew dodging icebergs crossing Bering Strait.

Suddenly the old man shouted, "Noonaveyit!" which we were to learn means that several walrus were on the ice. Had they been in the water he would have said, "Azougrakh." If only one were on the ice, it would be "Noonaveik." In their unwritten language they have eight or nine single words to describe walrus, their actions and location.

I had counted twelve rifles in the boat, all old and rusty. At the old man's shout each Eskimo grabbed the one he had placed handy and pumped a cartridge into the barrel.

I didn't know the language, but there was no mistaking the actions. There were walrus somewhere but I couldn't see them. That was because I was looking for them in the water. Then on a block of ice looming out of the fog I saw a cluster of five or six huge dark animals only two or three hundred feet away. They threw up their heads and their long white tusks glistened against their dark-brown hides. I started shooting pictures but didn't dare stand because the gunners lay low and motionless as the boat, at half throttle, glided directly toward the walrus.

They saw us but, probably having poor vision, appeared to be unable to make out what was approaching.

At about 150 feet the guns opened fire and the big animals panicked. The lucky and the wounded slid into the water. One lay dead and, as the bow of the boat slid up on the ice, two Eskimos jumped out, drew their knives with the foot-long blades and started to cut off the walrus' head, leaving a headless wild animal weighing more than a ton to drift off on a block of ice. But let's not pass judgment on this carnage yet.

A herd of twelve or fifteen walrus was waiting on a nearby block of ice—apparently not sufficiently alarmed from the melee to flee.

As the guns roared again, a large tusk snapped in half from a bad or unlucky shot. The broken tusk flew high in the air as the startled bull plunged into the water. Another bull lay dead on the ice. A third, dead or mortally wounded, slid slowly off the ice. The hunters started for him with the harpoon, but too late. He sunk into the sea as dead walrus usually do.

While this was going on, one Eskimo, tall and wiry, stood on the ice scanning the water in practically all directions at once. A more alert man I have never seen. Then he shouted, "Get a paddle in the water."

Suddenly realizing he was shouting at me, I looked into the water beside me and saw three pairs of shining tusks backed by tons of ferocious young bull walrus coming full speed at the very spot in the boat where I was sitting.

Waylaying that onslaught with a flimsy paddle seemed as ridiculous to me as elephant hunting with a BB gun.

In the instant it took me to decide that retreat was the wiser course of action, the long lean Eskimo had bounded off the ice into the boat and was pumping lead into the water beside me. None too soon, either, because they were within five feet when his bullets changed their course.

The head and gleaming tusks of another bull walrus which lost his life for his two front teeth lay at my feet as we again set out on the foggy sea to Diomede.

Two and a half hours after leaving Wales and having had considerable excitement along the way, the lean Eskimo, who was also compassman and navigator, stood, pointed straight ahead and turned with a proud smile to speak to the old man and Captain Tommy.

I saw nothing for awhile. Then what appeared to be fog took the form of a nearly vertical-sided mountain with valleys of snow. In the strong and complex currents of Bering Strait, with a strong cross wind, we had traveled 27 miles through fog, dodged icebergs, killed two walrus and not only located the tiny island, but hit the exact spot on the southwest corner which led to our destination on the west side.

Such navigation might appear to be sheer luck, but they do it so frequently that considerable skill must be involved. Open water is located by dark sky. Over ice the sky is light. In fog they may locate the island by the smell of the large colonies of nesting birds or fire a shot and listen for the echo.

At long last we were about to visit the primitive Eskimo village of Diomede.

Little Diomede Island

That Little Diomede Island could be inhabited by anything other than cliff-nesting birds seems incredible. It is a 1308-foot-high mountain of rock less than seven miles in circumference. Much of the shoreline rises out of the water as a precipitous cliff.

As we cruised along the cliffs in the skin boat which had brought us from Wales, murres, puffins and auklets by the thousands left their rocky perches and flew overhead.

We swung north along the west side of the island where the sheer cliffs gave way to steep jagged rocks. There, clinging to the mountainside, was the village of Diomede, the home of fifteen families totaling 70 people. A shot was fired from the boat as we approached and soon the entire population was on the beach to welcome the return of the hunters.

It seemed unbelievable that human life could be sustained on a tiny island of barren rock until I realized that for the Eskimos, as for the birds, it was the sea which provided the resources which sustained life. A few leaves, herbs and berries are collected by Eskimos high in the mountain. But almost everything they eat, wear or build boats from comes from the sea. When the sea fails to yield its bounty to the hunters, food is scarce and starvation is within the memory of the islanders.

The sea is not only the great provider, but the sole disposal system. All unwanted material, from human waste to empty oil barrels, is dumped into the sea.

For days I have been trying to understand the Eskimo's attitude toward the animals and birds which sustain him. I have not totally succeeded. It may not be possible for one reared in the traditions of conserva-

Jim Kimball entering Eskimo "door." (Little Diomede)

tion, sportsmanship and the love of wild things for what they are to ever comprehend the Eskimo's attitude toward wild animals.

The Eskimo is a hunter—a predator akin to the hawk, wolf or fox. He gives little thought to the welfare of his prey. He concerns himself only with how to get it. Like other predators, he kills so that he may survive.

At various seasons of the year he hunts seals, walrus, polar bears and whales. He traps, nets and shoots birds and collects their eggs. He doesn't worry too much about tomorrow—to say nothing of next year or of a succeeding generation.

Conservation and sportsmanship are recent human attitudes accepted by our civilization. Should we expect to find them in Eskimos who are about in the position that our American Indians were in 75 years ago?

But Eskimos are full American citizens with all the obligations, as well as the rights and privileges of you and me. Should they be permitted to take birds and their eggs or shoot waterfowl in the spring? Before answering, let us remember that this has been the source of their existence for countless generations.

John Iyapana at home by seal oil lamp. (Little Diomede)

The Seal Oil Lamp

The number of auklets and their eggs taken from the millions that nest on this island is an insignificant harvest and one that is fully utilized for human consumption. Laws should apply to all citizens alike, but should they deprive people of their food and employment and put them on charity?

*   *   *   *

Sitting at a table in the Diomede schoolhouse where we are living, I was writing and Breck was making beautiful paintings of auklets. He looked out the window to see an Eskimo lad bring down a kittiwake (small gull) with his slingshot. Because Breck likes to paint from live or freshly killed birds to get beak and foot colors before they fade, he wanted that kittiwake. So I rushed down and paid the happy boy a dime for his stoned quarry.

The bird was recovering rapidly as I brought him in. A moment after I handed him to Breck, the bird suddenly regurgitated from both ends simultaneously.

As I continue to write, the good professor is busy cleaning himself and the floor.

*   *   *   *

Yesterday morning was foggy but the Eskimos sensed walrus, so nearly all the men in the village took to sea in three skin boats. It seemed incredible that they would go out and expect to get back to the little island when you could not see a hundred yards through the fog.

After hunting all day and all night, two boats returned about seven this morning. One had 44 walrus, the other 20. Without a moment for sleep, the hunters ate, took on a new supply of gasoline and went out to hunt again. The third boat has not yet returned.

They think nothing of going several days and nights without rest. Sometimes they will hunt for a week with nothing more than the brief naps they may get in the boat. They admit that this is hard on them, but when walrus are in the area nothing else counts.

It is hard to imagine human beings more rugged than the Eskimo hunters. When they put out to sea in their skin boats, there is no scheduled return. If storms become too severe, they pull their boats up on the ice and wait. Sometimes it is a long cold wait.

According to our standards, Eskimos are wanton killers. By the time the children can toddle they are trying to kill any bird they see by throwing rocks or with slingshots.

One day Breck and I were standing on the beach beside a boat talking to some Eskimos. Breck spotted a red-necked loon out on the water and pointed it out to the Eskimos. One of them picked up his rifle and shot at it—missing by an inch or two. He didn't want the bird, just wanted to see if he could hit it.

*   *   *   *

Yesterday afternoon (June 14) the fog lifted. It was bright, calm and warm (45-50 degrees). Breck and I had tried midday bird photography with little success. The Eskimos told us why. In July, when they have started to nest, birds will be around the rocks all day, but in June their days are spent on the sea and they return to the rocks about 6 p.m.

We started climbing the mountain behind the village at five o'clock. Breck carried a packsack of movie equipment and I had two 35 mm. cameras (one for color and one for black and white) plus a variety of telephoto lenses and related equipment.

We got separated and I spotted an Eskimo climbing the mountain with a bird net. I got over to him and found it was Raleigh Ozenna. Could I follow and take pictures? "Yes." How close to him could I be? "Ten or eight feet, maybe." How far was he going? "Little way up."

I thought I could climb, but he lit out at two or three times my best speed. Soon he was out of sight but I kept right on climbing.

About the time I decided he had successfully demonstrated the inadequacies of the white man, I looked far up the mountainside and saw him waving me on.

The puffing and panting remains of me arrived in time to see Ozenna arranging his decoy device. A thin piece of oogruk hide, called Eskimo rope, was attached to one rock stretched over the top of a short stick on a higher rock and down to another anchor rock. Fastened along this were short pieces of thin thong.

A few feet away a half circle of rocks had been built up to form a blind. Raleigh squatted in his blind with his net which was a strange ob-

Eskimo girl with crested auklet. (Little Diomede)

long hoop, about six inches by sixteen inches, attached to a thin 14-foot handle.

As the birds came over, he deftly scooped a crested auklet out of the air. He took the bird to his decoy arrangement, threaded one of the short thongs through the bird's nostrils and tied it. There it hung by its bill, flapping violently, while he went back to his blind. The first ten birds caught were hung in this manner. He never attempted to catch the much more numerous but smaller least auklets.

After catching a few more, he grinned at me and said, "You want to try?" I couldn't resist. Whereupon I thoroughly disgraced the white race.

I swung the net at every bird, big or little, that came by and never even touched one. It was like trying to hit a Ping-Pong ball coming at thirty miles an hour with a paddle attached to a 14-foot pole. Finally, in a particularly awkward maneuver, I knocked down half of his blind and gave up.

As he continued to pick birds out of the air with ease, I now appreciated the great skill involved. If the Minnesota Twins would sign three of these Eskimos for the outfield, the pennant would be assured.

When I asked what was the greatest number of birds he had caught in an evening I got the usual obscure Eskimo answer, "Sixty—sometimes a hundred or more."

I had not planned to make the 1308-foot climb to the top of Little Diomede, but it was our first and only clear day and Raleigh Ozenna had already led me up a long way so I kept on climbing. It was a rewarding experience.

From the top of the crags on the summit I looked to the east and saw the snowcapped mountains of Alaska. To the west, across the international date line, the rugged coast of Siberia could be seen over the top of Russian-owned Big Diomede Island. The Pacific Ocean lay to the south and the Arctic Ocean was to the north.

I stood on the only spot on this whole earth from which you can see two continents, two oceans, two days and the two major world powers.

Far below lay the scarcely visible village which was home to seventy of the most rugged people on earth.

Murres

The top of Little Diomede. The only place in the world where you can see two oceans, two major world powers, two days, two continents. (Picture taken with self-timer.)

By the time I climbed back down the mountain to the village of Diomede it was midnight. Pointing my camera due north, I photographed the sun at its lowest point and still nearly half visible above the horizon. One more ambition achieved, I was seeing the midnight sun.

* * * *

Bones and muscles creaked as I rolled out of bed this morning. Trying to follow the Eskimo bird netter and climbing to the mountain peak yesterday were more than I was in condition for.

The one day of good weather had gone too. A strong north wind had brought 30-degree temperatures and floating ice was moving southward across the sea. The urge to remain inside and catch up on the writing was strong, but I had not yet photographed murres, parakeet auklets or puffins.

These birds occupy the vertical cliffs on the south end of the island. Inquiring how best to get there, the Eskimos gave me the usual vague and conflicting answers.

"Only way to go by skin boat." "Can walk along beach." "Can't walk beach." "Climb through rocks half way up." "Go over top and climb down."

Rollie netting birds.

That many answers you could get from the same Eskimo, so why ask more? This is the way with Eskimo talk and it is one of the many things about them I cannot fathom. I don't think they are lying—not in the sense that we consider lying. Sometimes they may not understand; sometimes they may be joking; sometimes they may be giving a bad answer because it was improper for you to ask the question and sometimes I just don't know. If your question implies an answer, that is the answer you will get. So you learn to phrase questions very objectively.

I decided to reach the cliffs by climbing through the rocks half way up.

Did I say this was a tiny island? I take it all back. For hours and hours I scrambled over, under and around the great jagged rocks of which this island is composed and never did get to the south end. But I did get far enough to find some of the vertical cliffs and photograph puffins and murres—not the best pictures, perhaps, but I feel no urge to return. One day is enough clinging to the rocks, switching lenses and waiting while an icy gale tries to blow you off into the sea.

Eskimo Boy

The two things I was most advised to take on this trip were sunglasses and mosquito dope. I haven't turned my ear flaps up yet and the most valuable items are long underwear and a heavy down-filled jacket.

The weather here in the Bering Strait is truly severe. While it may not fall below minus 35 to 40 degrees in winter, the warmest summer day may not exceed 60 degrees and the wind is nearly always howling.

I am convinced that during the last two days I have seen more birds than during the previous days of my life. Each evening they come from the sea by the millions to find shelter, chatter and make love among the rocks.

While climbing across the mountainside the air above is constantly filled with birds. They are perched by pairs and by dozens on every rock, and under the rocks they chatter, coo, chuckle and squawk. It seems the world has been taken over by the birds.

*   *   *   *

Eskimos are friendly, obviously have great affection for their children, speak with pride and respect about "our womans" and like to make jokes. Jimmy Iyapana is constantly telling me that the weather is not going to get better and I am never going to get off the island. He calls me the "Diomede Kid."

Here is an example of one of their jokes which was pretty good. I asked Aaron if the canvas they pulled up on the side of the big skin boats had a name.

"Yes," he said. "Canvas have name."

"What is it?" I persisted.

"We call it canvas."

Talking to John Iyapana who had been in the boat which just killed 44 walrus, we learned that only the tusks were brought in.

We pointed out that these 44 walrus plus 20 killed by the other boat meant that 64 walrus (100 tons of meat, blubber and hide) plus nearly as many more wounded were left to rot in the sea. We asked if this waste didn't bother him.

That this was waste had obviously never occurred to him. "That is good hunting," he said. "We need ivory to carve and sell. That is how we get money for gasoline, guns and fuel oil."

He was one of the best-informed Eskimos on the island. There was no language barrier, but though we tried for an hour to explain the waste, he felt not the slightest twinge of conscience.

His economics were direct and perfectly logical. He explained that bringing in one or two whole walrus would be a day's work while by taking only the ivory they get many. Walrus must be hunted during the short time they are available. Anyway, they already had enough cow walrus for food.

Walrus ivory is worth $2.25 per pound and a bull carries about fifteen pounds. The oozhook (baculum) is worth at least $10.

The law provides that each hunter may not take more than five walrus cows per year. There is no limit on the bulls. When cows are available the bulls are considered valuable only for their ivory because their meat is tough and their one and a half to four-inch-thick hides are less valuable. Walrus skin, including a thick layer of blubber called kokh, is highly prized as food. I watched one boat come in to Wales with the skin from a female walrus. There were ten men on the boat and the skin, weighing perhaps 400 pounds, was carefully divided into ten equal pieces.

One thing that disturbs me about walrus hunting is the guns that are used. If the animals are not killed almost instantly, they slide into the water and sink. The Eskimos are good shots and aim for the spine at the base of the brain. However, the boat is moving and the heads may be swinging.

When we left Wales for Diomede the boat captain asked if we had a large gun. No wonder. They had eleven rusty, beat-up .222's and one lever-action 30-30. The .222 is too small to be legally used to shoot deer in many states. A walrus weighs twenty times as much as a deer. A few Eskimos have 30-06 rifles. They all should have them when they hunt walrus.

Ivory carving is an art at which these Eskimos excel. Next to hunting it is their highest skill and their greatest source of pride as well as income. Every man at Diomede carves and last year their carvings brought the village an income of at least $8,000.

The Diomede Islanders and the King Islanders claim to be the best carvers and, surprisingly, neither claims to be better than the other. There

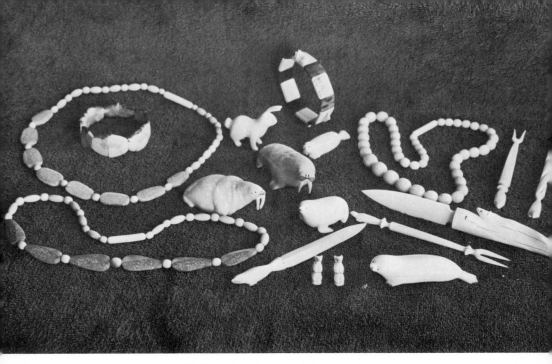

Eskimo jewelry carved from walrus ivory.

are a few expert carvers in Wales and other places, but not all carving is good.

I have seen only fine carving here at Diomede and when it is good it is not only unique, but genuinely artistic and beautiful. Bracelets, beads, buttons, letter openers, watchbands, figures for mounting on earrings, pickle forks, cocktail sticks, and charms are all carved from walrus tusk ivory. The figures of seals, polar bears and walrus are excellent.

Frequently the new white ivory is combined with jet black balene from whales' throats and rich brown antique ivory dug out of the ground where it may have aged for hundreds or thousands of years. They also use the beautiful brown ivory from the tusks of mammoths which have been extinct for ten or twelve thousands years.

I bought a couple of carved ivory pieces in Nome. Here, buying directly from the carvers, the prices are understandably more tempting—so tempting, in fact, that I may not have enough money to get home.

*   *   *   *

It isn't done much any more, but in former days the Diomede Eskimos would gather in the Kugree, a clubhouse similar to the Eskimo home but larger—about eighteen feet square, to work or tell stories. Here the women worked together preparing skins, making sealskin pants and parkas, Eskimo raincoats out of oogruk or walrus intestines, picking birds and the hundred other jobs classified as woman's work.

When men returned from a hunt all would gather in the Kugree to tell stories. The night before we left Diomede Island Albert related one of these tales.

It sounded so preposterous that we laughed and said, "You really don't believe that, do you?"

Albert smiled, turned his head a bit to one side and said, "They told it for the truth."

We shall never know what Albert believes, but here is the story. Decide for yourself.

Several Eskimos in a skin boat were hunting seal along the edge of the ice. The man in the bow speared a large seal and hung on to the rope. The seal was big and strong but the hunter, determined not to lose it, hung on and was pulled overboard.

He could not swim, but he was a smart man so, under water, he pulled himself hand over hand along the rope until he caught up to the seal. Now well under the ice, the seal was swimming so fast that there was a pocket of air behind his head.

The man put his arms around the seal and breathed from this pocket of air. Then he saw the seal coming up to a breathe hole in the ice, but the man could see it was too small for him to get through so he put his hand over the seal's nose so he could not get air.

Then the seal went to a larger breathe hole and the man crawled out and pulled the seal out after him.

Today I visited the largest home in Diomede which was originally the Kugree. It was a single room, as all of their homes are, but much larger.

A casual visitor to Diomede, if one could be casual, would say the town consisted of tiny shacks. He would be missing the real living quarters which are built into the rocky mountainside and are primarily subterranian. Many of the homes are about eight by ten feet, sometimes too low to stand in and there are no tables, chairs, beds or furniture of any kind other than the shelf along each wall.

The customary sleeping arrangements on the floor of an Eskimo home is for the father to be on one end, next is mother, then the youngest child, the next oldest, etc. The line may be long because families are frequently large.

To get into the large home, I went through a twenty-foot tunnel about two and a half feet wide and three and a half feet high. At the end I stood up to find my head and shoulders poking through a hole in the floor of the dwelling. The hole was eighteen inches in diameter and trimmed with walrus ivory. The room was lighted by a single window in the ceiling. This ceiling was supported by great arching whale ribs.

Because there was no furniture in the room, it seemed quite spacious. It was warm, clean and comfortable. Mrs. Okpealuk, now very old and blind, sat in the corner by the seal oil lamp. These lamps were long the sole source of light, heat for warmth and heat for cooking.

The one concession to the modern age was a gasoline stove in the middle of the floor. It was amazing how much larger the room appeared than it really was. So, if your home seems crowded, just throw out the furniture and sit, sleep, sew, cook, eat and play on the floor as the Eskimos have done for hundreds of years.

Later I visited and photographed the home of John Iyapana. Except for its smaller size, it was identical to the Kugree. John said his home provided ample room and required less heat. He also pointed out that his tunnel was a little higher, making it easier to enter.

As we talked, Mrs. Iyapana popped up through the hole. In a few minutes she brought out the table, which was a three-foot square board standing four inches above the floor. Two boys popped up through the hole and we had tea and a snack. As the boys left, one picked up the little white pot from under the shelf and relieved himself. Not having been decreed taboo by his civilization, this was as natural as taking a drink of water.

It was truly a warm, light, comfortable home and not the least crowded. Sitting on the floor seemed perfectly natural and tables, chairs or dressers would have been quite out of place. All necessities of life are in the room. Surpluses are stored in the attached little shack.

These people do not use eating utensils, but concede that spoons became a necessity when they started eating cereal.

Eskimo home—under the rocks. (Little Diomede)

In Diomede the ancient custom of sharing practically everything is still followed. If there is any food in the village, everyone eats. When the hunters come home villagers come to the beach to get what they need, including the precious ivory.

How does one go about teaching that the white man's greedy customs and efforts to outdo and outpossess his neighbor are superior and more Christian?

The village of Diomede would be considered a slum by our standards, but it is not a slum. It is in keeping with the Eskimo culture and traditions —many of them proudly preserved. Their homes are functional and practical in a country where fuel is scarce and expensive and temperatures are always low. These people have poverty only in the gadgetry that our society has decreed essential to a high standard of living. They lead a life of great variety, hunting and working tirelessly at times and working not at all at other times, and none is richer or poorer than his neighbor. It makes one wonder. What are we struggling for?

*   *   *   *

Superstition strongly influenced Eskimo lives in the past. They feared the return of the dead, and no matter how well one was liked in life, he was not wanted back in any form after death.

The deadly game—kids jumping sea ice. (Little Diomede)

When one died, no member of the family was permitted to sew, comb his hair or swing on ropes during the mourning period because this might pull the dead back. Hoods had to be kept over mourners' heads or they might lose their hearing, and if one picked plants, he would lose his fingernails.

Perhaps there was some conservation in their superstitions. If one disturbed a rare marbled murrelet on its nest, he would develop shoulder trouble. The eyes were cut out of a seal before it was butchered so it could not see who cut it up because seal were reincarnated as either some sea animal or a wolf. Therefore, it might attack the one who butchered it on either land or sea.

One man told us that all Eskimo superstitions were now gone, and I guess most of them are. But early this morning an Eskimo brought in a dovekie which he caught while netting auklets. He said it was bad luck to kill them. Breck was glad to get the bird because there were few, if any, records of them here.

One interesting bird we found in abundance is the little red phalarope which comes to land only in the Arctic to nest. It then returns to the

South Pacific near Australia where it remains on the ocean the rest of the year. This seems remarkable for such a tiny bird.

The great fear these Eskimos have of inadvertently landing on Russia's Big Diomede Island in the fog is not superstition. It springs from a serious incident. We have heard numerous accounts of this incident which varied widely in the telling. Last night we got the story from Albert Iyakuk and he should have the facts straight because he, along with his wife and two-year-old son, was involved.

Some of the Diomeders and most of their ancestors were born in Siberia or on Big Diomede Island. Occasionally they would return to visit relatives.

In 1947 or 1948, two skin boats carrying seventeen Diomeders set out for Siberia and stopped at Big Diomede to have their passports checked. They had not learned that Russia had ruled against further visits.

At Big Diomede the Russians took them into custody and held them for 52 days. Albert said they were put into tents and fed fish soup once a day. They were in bad shape when finally released. Some were sent to the hospital and it is said that one later died of T.B.

"Do you still have relatives in Siberia, Albert?" I asked.

"Did have, but no more—no more," Albert answered, and then laughed. Albert always laughs at a tragic situation.

He sat silent for a moment as his mind wandered back. Then he said, "I thought we not going back here no more." He laughed again.

Since that time no one knows whether there are still Eskimos living on Big Diomede Island and there is no contact with those in Siberia.

*   *   *   *

So many exciting things could hardly happen in one day. But the day started at 4 a.m., or perhaps it started the night before when Albert Iyahauk, the Diomede storekeeper, paid us a visit.

Breck and I had climbed over much of Little Diomede Island, photographed Russian Big Diomede Island and the Siberian coast, seen millions of birds and collected one or two of several species of birds for Breck to paint and to prepare scientific skins. We had talked to many of the seventy inhabitants of this most primitive village, got well acquainted with some, had given speeches at the school and photographed the people, dwellings and customs of this pretwentieth-century village. We were ready to leave.

But as Jimmy kept telling me, "You never know—maybe you here another month. All depends on weather."

I had dropped in at Albert's house for a short visit and was served tea. It was an honor, I thought, to have him return the call so quickly. These Eskimos had been sizing us up for a week and Albert's visit meant, I hoped, that we were considered neither rich suckers nor something worse. They are frequently suspicious that visitors are scheming to sneak over the three miles to Russia's Big Diomede—It has happened.

After two hours of most interesting talk, Albert peered out the window at the screaming gale stirring the angry Arctic Sea and said, "Think weather get better. Maybe we go Wales tomorrow. Take you."

"Fine," we said. "What time should we be ready?"

His typical Eskimo reply was, "Maybe afternoon, maybe two in morning. When weather is right."

We awakened to a pounding on the window on the second story of the schoolhouse where we slept.

Opening the window, we found John Iyapana at the top of the ladder. The schoolhouse door had been locked.

"You gonna go?" he asked.

We looked at the boat on the beach. It was loaded and ready, and miraculously the sea had calmed as Albert predicted. We looked at our watches. It was 4 a.m. We went.

The Eskimos had become intrigued with our interest in birds and for the past few days they had been bringing in interesting specimens brought down with their long-handled nets.

As we crawled into the 32-foot skin boat which I so admired, John said, "You wanna see birds—you gonna see lotsa, lotsa, lotsa birds today. We gonna take you Fairway Rock."

It is something to see, this Fairway Rock. It is not big enough to be called an island, but it is a great towering, jagged, craggy rock. It is a super devil's tower jutting up from the floor of the sea in Bering Strait to a height of 534 feet above the sea.

The north side, on which the Arctic morning sun shone, was painted green with moss, and on the narrow ledges sat tens of thousands of murres, auklets and puffins.

Our obliging Eskimo voyageurs considerately piloted the skin boat around the island as our cameras clicked and whirred.

A half hour before we had reached the rock on this bright clear day, Albert had said, "Looks like gonna snow." We were two-thirds around the rock when the sun disappeared and it snowed—not just a few flakes. It really snowed on this eighteenth day of June and it got cold.

We headed south from the rock rather than northeast toward Wales so we knew we were in for another Eskimo hunt.

When Eskimos sight game they forget their English, speak excitedly in Eskimo and use sign language. Of the seven Eskimos in the boat, two to four of them would be looking through binoculars at any one time. They are nearly always standing and frequently standing, with remarkable stability, on the seats.

Those in the front signal the man at the motor to avoid hitting floating ice. If there is not an immediate response to hand signals for right, left, fast or slow, they know their signal has not been noted and they jump slightly two times. This barely perceptible jarring of the boat alerts the man at the motor.

I didn't make out most of the signals, but if they touch their pants, which are made of sealskin, and point—it means a seal has been sighted. Touching fingers of one hand on the back of the other means the game they see is on top of the ice.

Suddenly there was excited Eskimo chatter. They had spotted a seal in the water. All that was visible was the round top of the seal's head, looking like a partially submerged beach ball.

The shots are long and difficult from a moving boat. They missed. The seal submerged and minutes later it came up just as far away but in the opposite direction. This continued and reminded me of trying to kill a crippled bluebill duck.

They hit one! It lay floating in the water as the boat headed for it at top speed. Twenty feet before we were close enough to throw the spear, it sank.

Disgustedly, Albert said, "Spring seal sink!" Apparently this is not a problem in the fall when the fat seal float.

Then John made a sign and pointed. For the enlightenment of Breck and me he said, "Ribbon seal on ice," and gave us the look which says, "It's as good as in the boat."

At half throttle or less the boat glided quietly straight toward the target. When the seal raised its head, John's rifle spoke and the head dropped. This seal has value for food, oil and hide, so it was quickly loaded into the boat and we were hunting again.

Before long the sign of walrus on ice was given. Nothing excites an Eskimo's hunting instinct as much as walrus. These men had killed hundreds, probably thousands of walrus, but their expressions and actions showed their never-dying thrill of the chase.

This was a lone animal on a block of ice. Its head suddenly rose and more suddenly fell as a clean kill was made.

At first the Eskimos were surprised to see it was a cow because they move north through the Bering Strait first and only bulls had been seen for several days.

Then they saw it was a very old and probably sick animal, so only the ivory was taken.

It was snowing harder again and the wind came up. The sea was both rolling and choppy. The canvas on the windward side of the boat was raised. In an hour we were in Wales.

*   *   *   *

Eskimos and walrus are the two things I keep thinking most about. You can hardly think about one without the other.

After talking of John Burns I should be less concerned about the walrus slaughter, but I can't help being somewhat emotional about killing animals weighing two tons to obtain fifteen pounds of ivory.

Burns is a biologist with the Alaska Fish and Game Department. A former track athlete, he has won the respect of the Eskimos by living with them in their homes for months at a time. He works with them, helps them hunt, lives as they live and eats what they eat. The Diomede Islanders expressed a high regard for Burns.

Between 1870 and 1880 American whalers killed over 100,000 walrus. This stopped when whaling became uneconomical, but it had marked the beginning of the walrus decline.

Hunting continued by Soviets and Americans until after World War I. It is claimed that one American schooner took 1300 walrus. The lowest point in walrus numbers was reached in the late 1920s and the 1930s.

Since then walrus numbers have increased, especially during the last fifteen years. Now, with more and more Eskimos relying on relief, government dole and unemployment checks, fewer of them hunt, so the walrus harvest is decreasing.

Besides, walrus are polygamous animals and there appears to be an abundance of bulls. Between 65% and 70% of the animals now being killed are bulls. Hunters are limited to five cows each and this can easily be policed because only Diomede and King Islands need to be watched. Only here, apparently, have the Eskimos retained enough of their historic skill, courage and ability to navigate the ice-laden seas to kill many walrus.

So we must conclude that the walrus are in no danger. But walrus meat is worth 25 cents a pound wholesale in Nome and a chemical company will pay $150 each for hides. However, the walrus harvest in any one year is unpredictable and transportation to Nome would consume much of the profit.

Eight Eskimos in a skin boat would do well to bring in two whole animals in a day and they would have a lot of skinning and butchering to do. Hunting only for ivory, they may get 20 to 40 on a good day. Considering the economics, the favorable condition of the walrus herd and the Eskimo's point of view, killing for ivory, distasteful though it be, is not so easily condemned.

                    *   *   *   *

Why hawks such as the falcons do not nest on Diomede where food is abundant, and how the Arctic foxes managed to survive the winters on the island are two questions which had Dr. Breckenridge and me stumped until we talked to biologist John Burns.

He agreed that the rocky cliffs would make ideal nest sites for duck hawks, but he believed the winds were not to their liking. These birds are

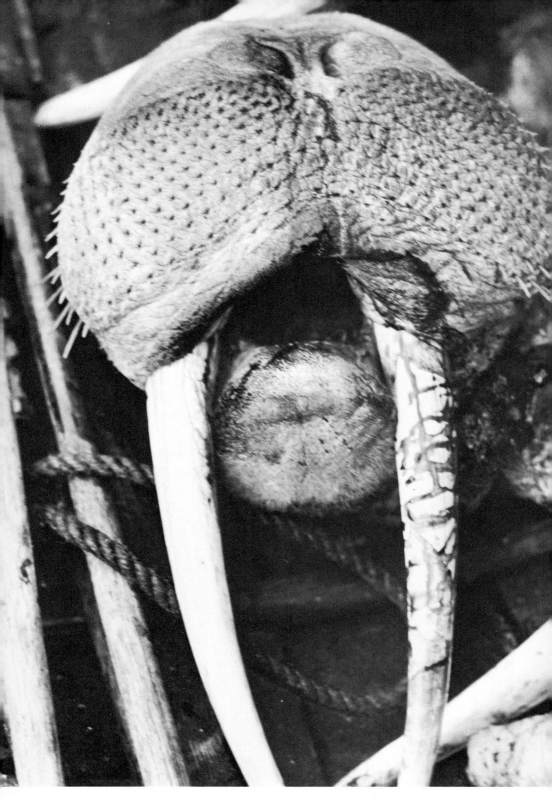

The face of a walrus. All the Eskimos want is the two front teeth.

superb fliers, but Burns believes they are not good at coping with the tricky, shifting air currents of great velocity occurring around the mountain.

We saw considerable Arctic fox sign on the island and realized the foxes must be living a life of plenty while the birds and their eggs were there. However, we could find no sign of lemmings, mice or ground squirrels and the Eskimos assured us there were none. How, then, did foxes survive the long winters?

When first asked this question, the Eskimos acted as if it were something they had not previously considered. After a little thought, they said the foxes stored away their winter supply of birds during the summer. One went into considerable detail, saying the foxes stored least auklets in one pile, crested auklets in another, etc. Then, during the winter, the fox would dig through the snow to the stored birds he wanted.

These Arctic foxes no doubt cache a number of birds, but I could not believe they would put up a supply which would last through the long Arctic winter.

When we asked Burns, the answer was immediate and no doubt correct. He said the Arctic fox is an animal of the ice. In winter he moves off the island and follows the polar bears. He said that every bear is followed by one or more foxes living off the remains of seal killed by the bears. Wolverine also follow the bears.

Eskimos are very fond of polar bear meat but are not getting as many bears as they once did. They blame the white airplane hunter.

I can't see that hunting polar bears from a plane requires any great skill or is very heroic or sportsmanlike. Hunters are flown out until they find a suitable bear. The plane lands on the ice, they pump him full of lead from high-powered rifles and proudly take home the head and hide for a trophy. About all this requires is money—lots of it.

Eskimos travel long distances on dangerous ice to get a bear and go out with their dog teams to pack him home. Some of the older men on King Island have killed sixty polar bears during their lives.

Burns was out on the ice one time with an Eskimo when they spotted a polar bear. All the Eskimo had was a .22 rifle, but he wanted the bear.

They got within forty feet of it. Considering the bear's heavy skull, a head shot with a .22 would be futile, so he shot at the chest. The little bullet apparently bounced off a rib and the bear raised up, scratching his chest and looking for the source of annoyance. The second shot entered his chest and the bear charged. A third shot in the neck brought him down. Burns made no attempt to conceal the fact that he was scared.

Before they had guns, Eskimos killed polar bears with spears. Bears also killed Eskimos.

The Eskimos learned that nearly all of the bears were right-handed —an important bit of knowledge when you are fighting with a spear and knife. Dogs were important aids in killing a bear.

One bear-killing technique was to harass the bear with dogs and aggravate him into a charge. As he approached, the Eskimo would throw a mitten into the air which would make the bear rear up. As he came down, the Eskimo would set his spear under his chest with its base on the ice. I'd rather buy pork chops at the supermarket.

Airplane hunters are probably killing or driving away many of the polar bears which were once available to Eskimos, but it seems unlikely that they are depleting the bear population. Being trophy hunters, they usually pass up the females and search for large males.

The range of these great white bears is circumpolar. They travel great distances and no one knows their numbers. Apparently they do not hibernate. The females go to land to have their young and remain there for two or three months. Other than this, their entire lives are spent on sea ice.

*   *   *   *

As would be expected, Alaska, being in the early stages of wildlife management, pays bounties. And nowhere is the political motive for bounty payments more obvious. A $3 bounty is paid on all species of hair seal, which are the only kinds found this far north. There are also bounties of $15 on wolverines, $30 on coyotes and $50 on wolves. That these bounty payments are purely a political vote-buying dole is best illustrated by the $50 wolf bounty.

According to the best available information, wolves are needed in Alaska to help hold down the excessive caribou herds of over half a million in the Arctic. Hoof rot is a serious contagious caribou disease and the limping animals that lag because of it are picked off by the wolves.

Wolf hunting is prohibited during some months. There is a limit of two a year and their pelts are worth $50. But the $50 bounty continues. Wolverine pelts are also worth $50, and in some areas there is a closed season on spotted seal, but still there is a bounty on their heads. Eskimo votes are important in Alaska.

Breck was especially eager to see and, if possible, photograph the white wagtail which may well be the rarest bird on the North American continent. Where did we locate this rare elusive bird after searching the Arctic tundra? Nesting inside a vacant Eskimo house in Wales. I took his picture "perched upon a windowsill." Too bad he didn't "have a yellow bill."

Back to Nome

Nome seemed plenty exciting on our first visit, but after seeing the primitive conditions on Wales and Diomede, hunting seal and walrus and seeing millions of birds, we thought returning to the relatively civilized community of Nome would be an anticlimax.

However, when we returned to Wales from Diomede the lagoon to the north where we had planned to camp out was still frozen over. The only place you can fly from Wales is back to Nome. So we caught the mail plane out.

While waiting for the plane at Wales I sat in the village native store and talked to the manager, Pat Ongtowasruk, an intelligent young Eskimo.

Somehow we got on the subject of drinking. I should interject that Eskimos drink for one purpose—to get drunk. Diomede, for example, is a peaceful, friendly little village when there is no liquor. But liquor, like everything else, is shared, and when there is booze in town I had been told that almost every adult gets drunk. Drinking is also recognized as a serious problem when villagers go to Nome.

I tried to explain to Pat how different drinking is with us. I told him that most of the people I know drink, but few of them ever get drunk. I tried to explain moderate social drinking—the one cocktail before dinner.

He couldn't comprehend putting a bottle away before it was empty. He could see no sense in it, but he was certainly interested. He would look at me with those big dark Mongolian eyes and say, "Talk some more."

The second visit to Nome was much more interesting than we had anticipated. We got a taste of real northern hospitality.

Panning gold (Nome)

Breck, demonstrating his professorial prerogative to be absentminded, had lost his traveler's checks. No place in Nome handled them and it was not only Sunday, but the midst of the two-day Midnight Sun Festival.

By telephone we finally located one official of the Nome Miners and Merchants Bank, Jack Carpenter. He not only opened the bank and solved our financial problems, but spent the whole day showing us around.

There was an Eskimo dance and the famous blanket toss. One attraction I had never seen before was a three and a half mile raft race down the Nome River. Fourteen rafts made of everything from inner tubes and Hylex bottles to beer cans staged a spectacular show. Anything went—including upsetting the other fellow's raft. A thousand people watched and the prize provided by the Junior Chamber of Commerce was a fur-lined stainless steel honey bucket.

Gold gave birth to Nome. With mining gone, government checks and tourists are its only visible means of support.

Returning from the raft race, we stopped to see and photograph the world's second largest gold dredge. Its size defies description. It is the length of two football fields and weighs 3,600 tons. Working in permafrost, the ground had to be thawed to depths of 90 feet before the dredge could dig.

The giant dredge, which cost over $1½ million to build in 1940, operated for one year and shut down because of the war. There are rumors that it more than paid for itself in that year.

It was put to work again in 1948 and operated until 1962. Then, because operation costs greatly increased while the product, gold, was held at a constant value of $35 per ounce by the government, operation is no longer economically possible. We were told that the price of gold would have to go up to at least $70 per ounce before mining could start again.

We met Carl Glavinovich who is said to know more about gold mining than anyone in northern Alaska. Asked if there were still gold to be mined, Glavinovich said yes and then proved it beyond any doubt.

He put a couple of shovels of sand and gravel into a pan, carried it to a nearby pool of water and started washing. Soon the bright flakes of color began to show. In fifteen minutes the stones and sand were gone and about $3 worth of placer gold remained in the pan.

Eskimos are, in my opinion, a rather handsome race and the kids are the cutest things imaginable. They are friendly and unafraid, too. Their round, brown faces with big black eyes beam at you from under silky black hair or out of fur-trimmed parkas.

At Wales they got to know me and would come running and shouting, "Hi, Jim! Hi, Jim!" But some mischievous Eskimo must have told them a mean trick because one day the little rascals came running to me shouting, "Hi, father! Hi, father!" This is my first trip to Alaska.

* * * *

KOTZEBUE, ALASKA

Kotzebue, north of the Arctic Circle, was our next stop. This village is booming with the construction of large schools by the U. S. Bureau of Indian Affairs. Many Eskimos are making good wages, but with others, hunting and fishing goes on as usual. Dogs are everywhere patiently waiting the end of the brief summer to obtain relief in the beloved harness from their short chains.

Kotzebue is a major jumping-off place for non-Eskimo polar bear hunters. There are two or three small hotels and bush pilots are for hire.

Fish caught in nets are an important source of Eskimo food. Trout, salmon and tom cod hang from drying racks throughout the village.

An amusing amalgamation of the old and new cultures was depicted on the beach. Eskimo women, wearing blue jeans under dresslike native parkas, skillfully butchered a large oogruk and a small seal.

A cold Arctic sea wind swept across the beach. Comfortable in my down jacket and winter underwear, I shivered in sympathy as the bare-handed women handled the cold blubber and skinned and carved with their ulus.

Then one woman went into the house and brought forth coffee in a new Pyrex pot. Not even bothering to seek protection from the bitter wind, they sat beside the oily carcasses having their coffee break and chatting like a bevy of office girls.

The federal cost of building a fine, modern high school in a place as isolated as Kotzebue must be great, but we were pleased to see it. If the Eskimo is to join our society, and he has little alternative, education is his

Eskimo women skinning an oogruk with their ulus (circular knives) — Kotzebue.

greatest need. We talked to a fine, intelligent high school lad who demonstrated a cordial, friendly manner and grammatical excellence.

But good teachers are not readily available for isolated little villages. Some are dedicated to helping the Eskimos, but too many who come up from the states sign on for two years of good civil service pay and the opportunity to hunt, fish and see the Arctic.

Breck never steps out the door, even to cross the street, without binoculars hanging around his neck. He might see some rare bird.

Today I saw him walking back to Kotzebue from a birding hike with an Eskimo boy in tow. I wondered what was going on because, much as "The Birdman" likes these people, he can't quite forgive the Eskimo lads for shooting at every living bird.

As we met he introduced me to the boy and said, "I made a target for him and taught him to shoot at it. He is going to teach the other kids and they will make a game of shooting targets instead of birds."

The boy beamed an expression of total agreement.

"Are you a good shot?" I asked the boy.

"Not very."

"Can you hit that beer can down on the beach?"

In a lightning draw his slingshot came out of his hip pocket as he stooped for a stone.

"Ping!"—The beer can jumped a foot.

Well, Professor Breckenridge, that boy may shoot targets, but he was born to hunt and I wouldn't advise one of your precious red phalaropes to get within range of his hip pocket.

Point Barrow

This was our day to visit the top of the world, to see the midnight sun at its highest from the most northerly point on the North American continent. The C47 plane, loaded with 25 tourists plus Breck and me, lifted off the Kotzebue airport at noon.

In a couple of hours we were over Point Barrow. But between us and this most northern United States village were low clouds. We could not land.

Beneath the sun and above the clouds we circled, waiting. Twice the pilot tried to land but just as we began to see land or ice—too close beneath us—the motors roared and we were up again.

Then the "Fasten Your Seatbelts" sign lit up and it was announced that we would make an alternative landing at Umiat.

Whoever heard of Umiat? Finally I located this speck on the map. It was back in the desolate interior of the Arctic, 185 miles southeast of Point Barrow. The only happy person on the plane was Professor Breckenridge. He would find out what birds inhabited such a place.

Umiat exists only because our U. S. Navy has been exploring the area for oil and apparently found it.

In the short time we were there Breck and I located nine species of birds including one from Siberia and, believe it or not, a big fat robin. We both watched him carrying a mouthful of food to a nest and young. This may be as far north as robins have ever been recorded.

It was cold. The ponds were covered with ice. Everything was frozen. Why would a robin which could be nesting in your elm tree and enjoying a Minnesota late June while pulling worms from your lawn be nesting in this frozen expanse of brown land and white snow and ice?

With radio word that weather had cleared at Point Barrow, we were flying again.

On these flat lands north of the Brooks Range of mountains we saw the Arctic polygons which are a characteristic of the tundra. They look like the bottom of a shallow, muddy marsh which has dried and cracked in the sun, but each many-sided form is as big as a house and covered with vegetation.

As far as you can see the landscape is dotted with ponds, large and small. Superficially, it resembles the prairie pothole county of the Dakotas. It looks like a great waterfowl production area, but, except for a few eiders, no ducks nest here.

We saw several small herds of Barren Grounds Caribou and their trails. Anything that travels through this county leaves a trail that lasts for years. For a long time there were only caribou trails. Then, as we drew near Point Barrow, I saw trails left by dog sleds and then by snowmobiles.

Barrow is the largest Eskimo village in Alaska, but it resembles Kotzebue more than the primitive villages such as Wales. There are white people, small hotels, churches and junky cars. Except for the short road to the airport, there seems to be no place for the dilapidated junkers called automobiles to travel.

There are various kinds of trucks, all with four-wheel drives and amazingly large tires for traveling over the loose beach gravel on which Barrow is built. Many of the large tires were taken from DC-3 airplanes.

The other vehicles are a variety of weird devices which run on rubber tracks and can no doubt travel over the ice and tundra.

I have always wanted to see the sun at midnight on one of the longest days of the year from the northernmost place on the continent. I expected it to be above the horizon, but it was high in the sky—as if it were 3 p.m.

For 82 days the sun never sets here and for two months in midwinter it never rises. It is only a little more than a thousand miles to the North Pole. Our little hotel room had a north window and no shade. It was so bright that I had to lay a sock over my eyes before I could get to sleep.

Midnight at Barrow, Alaska

Lemming

We didn't spend much time in the village as we were eager to visit the Arctic Research Laboratory (ARL) administered by the University of Alaska for the Office of Naval Research.

We were delighted and considerably honored when the ARL director, Dr. Max C. Brewer, authorized us to stay with them for a few days.

The laboratory, three miles northeast of the village, is a small town in itself where research of various kinds is conducted by universities and visiting scientists from all parts of the world. Normally, 70 scientific projects are in progress each year.

I learned about lemmings—those strange little Arctic animals which become tremendously abundant and, according to legend, make mass suicide marches into the sea.

Mouselike and the size of a small gopher, with a very short tail, lemmings are extremely cyclic. Every four or five years they build up to great numbers and then disappear. They are at near peak numbers now and Breck and I saw them everywhere, darting out from under one snow patch to hide under another. Where the ground is bare you can see that it is covered with a network of runways where these nonhibernating animals have spent the winter. The grassy vegetation on the peatlike soil is almost completely devoured and you wonder how anything could survive on so little food.

These defenseless little animals seem to have been created to be eaten. Their only guard against extinction is their phenomenal ability to reproduce. Permanently frozen ground precludes them from digging holes, so when snow melts they become easy prey for anything that is hungry.

At the low of the cycle there will be only one lemming on twenty acres. Three men running traps during the entire summer of 1958 caught only one lemming. It seems incredible that they will increase in four years until there are 400 of them on each acre.

During the cycle rise, lemmings will have two or three litters of seven or eight young during the summer. Nor do they stop reproducing when the short summer ends. They have two or three additional smaller litters in the winter. Further increasing this progression, the young reach breeding age and start having young of their own when only sixteen days old.

Major summer predators are the gull-like jaegers, snowy owls and weasels. In winter they are eaten by foxes. Our common red fox is found way up here at the top of the world, but the Arctic fox is more common.

A fox catches lemmings by walking stealthily on top of the snow until, by sound or smell, a lemming is located. He then leaps high in the air and with all four feet close together, comes down through the snow on top of his prey.

Some of this locating must be done by the fox's sense of smell because they can locate the lemmings dead or alive. Researchers placed 400 dead lemmings under the snow in the fall. By spring every one had been eaten—mostly by foxes. In some cases the foxes dug through twenty inches of snow to find them.

Dr. Frank Pitelka from the University of California, here studying the population dynamics of lemmings, puts no stock in the tales of their making mass suicide migrations to the sea. At population peaks lemmings do move but, according to Pitelka, in no particular direction. In Norway, which he has visited, he believes the nature of the terrain may have funneled many, by accident, into the fjords and the sea.

Why do the number of lemmings rise and fall so drastically? Why are they a thousand times more abundant one year than another? In other words, why are there cycles? No one yet knows and it is something that needs to be known. The quest for fundamental biological knowledge goes on.

About Eskimos

The Barrow area is by far the most utterly bleak, desolate and foreboding land I have ever seen. When it is thus now under the never-setting sun I can scarcely imagine what it is like in midwinter during the months of lightless days when the sun never rises.

It is hard to imagine how the polar bear, Arctic fox and wolverine survive the winters. That human beings have lived here for countless generations defies imagination.

I must keep reminding myself that they live not from the barren land, but from the bounty of Neptune's ocean. However, even now, past the longest day of the year, shore ice extends out for miles and most of the ground is covered with snow.

I wanted to get a dog team to take me out to the open sea, but learned that shore ice could break away at any time. I have no desire to float over the North Pole on a king-sized ice cube.

The spring whaling season is past, but it has been a good year for whales at Point Barrow. They got ten last fall and two this spring. Most of these are the large bowhead whales and some are the even larger blue whales, the biggest mammals that ever lived.

When a whale is killed and pulled up on the ice, the Eskimo women come out and go to work. Within two days it has been cut up and hauled away. The black balene from the throats of these toothless whales combines beautifully with the white walrus ivory in making jewelry.

I came to Alaska to learn about Eskimos. I have learned to admire them—some for what they still are; others for what they must have been.

The noble savage? Perhaps. They are as rugged, rough and tough as they are friendly. They used to travel the seas between villages at King Island, Diomede, Siberia, Wales and possibly even Point Barrow to pick fights. They didn't set out for conquest or to intentionally kill each other. But they would steal women, which were always in short supply, and possibly take a child or two. Sometimes Diomeders would join King Islanders in fighting the Siberian Eskimos. Or they might join the Siberians in fighting the King Islanders. Anything for a good fight.

I certainly do not claim to understand Eskimos. It would require years for people spawned of such widely differing cultures to really understand each other. But a few things appear obvious.

The Eskimo culture probably reached its pinnacle in Bering Strait where hunting required courage and skill but was productive enough to leave leisure time—time to be creative and develop skills and art.

That this rich Eskimo culture is doomed seems a certainty. The younger generation can no longer build skin boats or speak the language, and very few are even learning the Eskimo dances or how to carve ivory. A few years ago the population of Diomede was 140. Now it is 70, and the King Island village of 240 has dwindled to 15 hardy souls.

The lure of white man's civilization, his luxury, easy money and apparent soft living are bringing Eskimo culture to a rapid end. There is a saying here, "Easy money is ruining Alaska." It really means, "Easy money is ruining the Eskimo."

It is also said that the Eskimo is satisfied with "subsistence living." This is a nice way of saying that he is thriftless, lives from hand to mouth and accumulates nothing.

This should surprise no one. Eskimos place small value on material things and are probably happier for it. They have never practiced the accumulation of wealth or tried to be better off than their neighbors. Everything is shared.

Driftwood is plentiful along the beaches, but Eskimos do not gather and stockpile it for winter fuel because their relatives and neighbors would "borrow" it. This seems strange or unfair to us, but from the Eskimo's point of view we are saying, "Learn to be selfish and you can join our society."

Eskimos certainly do not like or respect us for giving them money, whether it be cash handouts or relief and unemployment checks. This is so obvious and so certain it makes one wonder if the United States' "give away" programs make friends anywhere.

If the Eskimos decide a man has plenty of money they feel perfectly justified in trying to get some of it, because no man needs so much.

Albert Iyahuk told me about two men who came to Diomede to hunt walrus. He said, "Two men came from Chicago. Got lotsa, lotsa money. I charge them $100 a day each. Two days they not get walrus. Ho! Ho! Then they say we pay $500 when get walrus. Next day both shoot walrus. Ho! Ho! Ho! They got lotsa money."

The less contact Eskimos have had with the white men the better we liked them and the more readily they accepted us. This was most noticeable in the children—which is usually the best place to look for honest answers. The friendly, beaming little faces, outstretched hands and offers to help carry bags were found in the remote little villages.

Assimilation of one race by another always means hardship and bitterness, but I believe it will be quick and relatively simple with the Eskimo. It is said that most bush pilots here have Eskimo wives and certainly a great many other white men do. There is little if any stigma attached to marrying an Eskimo. An example of this is found in Kotzebue where 14% of the residents are white, 25% are Eskimo and 61% are mixed.

This kind of assimilation, or absorption, appears to be far more successful and less of a problem than integration as we know it throughout our country.

Our religion sometimes baffles the Eskimo. Frequently three to five denominations will establish churches in one small village. The Eskimo concludes that if the white man cannot make up his mind about Christianity, how can he?

To have seen the Eskimo as he is today in the most primitive villages is one of the greatest experiences of my life. The outboard motor has replaced the sail and the gasoline stove is replacing the seal-oil lamp, but the true Eskimo culture is either still intact or within the memory of those to whom you talk.

In attempting to analyze another culture, the bigotry of one's own society becomes obvious.

Our society cringes at the thought of eating animal intestines. Why? We eat whole sardines and oysters. Who decided that muscles and liver were edible and intestines not? Is this logic or is it a very simple example of the many prejudices encompassed in our culture?

The wide gap between the Eskimo culture and ours makes misunderstanding understandable. Is it not logical to assume that misunderstandings between this nation and those of Europe and Asia are also partially the result of different cultural backgrounds, customs and prejudices?

Regardless of our effort to be tolerant, we feel superior to the Eskimos and, of course, in our environment we are. But were I dropped on a rocky Arctic Ocean island for the winter, I would certainly look for an Eskimo to keep me alive.

A pair of carved ivory walrus on the mantel and 300 color slides are my cherished mementos of the barren but exciting Arctic—of floating ice, countless birds, walrus, seals, tundra, beaming black-eyed kids, the midnight sun and the fascinating culture of a friendly, rugged people.

This diary would not be complete without a final word about my companion, Dr. W. J. Breckenridge—the great man with the one terrible fault. The genial professor's talents are widely known: artist, photographer, lecturer, author, museum director and Phi Beta Kappa captain of his tumbling team.

Naturally I assumed that one with such an imposing array of talents would possess some knowledge of the culinary art. But, alas, he is a worse cook than I. Together we learned that oogruk meat, walrus liver and seal liver were excellent when fried. So, though it amused the Eskimos, I didn't blame Breck too much for trying to fry a hunk of stringy, rubbery walrus meat which should have been boiled for two hours. But that a man of Breck's learning and resourcefulness can be content with a diet of grape-nuts and powdered milk is unforgivable.

PART III

THE PHILOSOPHICAL
HERMIT

My friend the Philosophical Hermit

What Good in a Bear?

Because my new friend, the Philosophical Hermit, does not want you to come to visit him, we agreed not to tell you his name nor in what remote spot in northern Minnesota his cabin is hidden away.

When I first saw the hermit walking down the trail from his cabin I knew in an instant that I was looking at a man who had spent most of his life in the woods. You could not tell just from his heavy beard or his bare feet, of course, but when you see a man literally gliding through the forest in a free hip-swinging stride, you know you are looking at a woodsman.

I don't know what one should expect when he arrives unannounced and is invited into a hermit's cabin. Whatever I expected, it was not what I saw.

At first glance, the cabin was obviously neat, clean, and in good taste. Then I perceived that everything in the room was not only handmade, but beautifully hand carved. Carved wolf tracks walked up a cabinet door on top of which sat a carved owl. Some cabinet doors were veneered with birch bark, others carved, and each hinge and latch was a hand-wrought masterpiece of metal. Most beautiful of all, perhaps, were the carved and inlaid stocks on his guns. It would be interesting to know what value a connoisseur of fine guns would place on these works of art.

In this log cabin one of the few concessions to 20th-century living could hardly be considered a modern device. It was a small hand mill with which friend hermit grinds all his meal and flour.

Yet, the most startling incongruity about this man who lives alone in the wilderness was not his appearance, his walk, his cabin, his carvings,

The Hermit with his Sally

his hand-wrought iron work nor his fine garden. It was his manner of speech. Somehow, you don't expect a hermit to have a full, resonant voice and an excellent vocabulary. It seemed so unfortunate that such an articulate man should be heard only by his little dog, Sally, that I finally convinced him to permit me to turn on my miniature tape recorder. The rest of this story is composed of bits of his statements during our conversation.

"How did I choose this place to live? Well, I used to work for the Forest Service in California as a lookout and trail builder. Each spring when the fire hazard was down I would take off and look for an unspoiled piece of country where I could settle down. Central Idaho looked pretty good, and northern Maine would have been all right if I hadn't seen the big country farther west. But, after ten years of search, I located this spot and knew it was what I wanted.

"I have not the slightest shred of interest in publicizing my wholly unremarkable self. I am not at all sure the views and opinions I undertake to expound are worth repeating. Certainly many of them lack perspective as I've only Sally with whom to discuss them, and though in many ways an admirable little dog and an excellent companion, she's rather weak at spotting faulty logic.

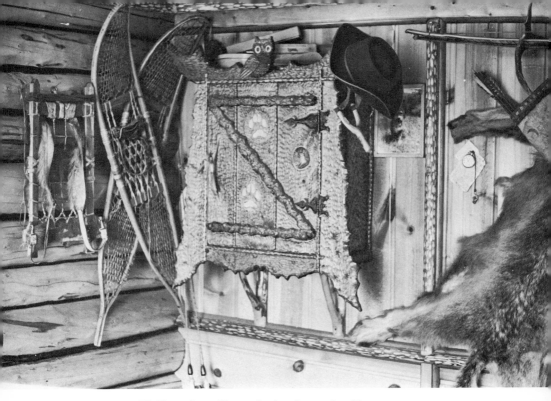

Wolf tracks walk up the hand-carved cabinet.

"During my formative years I read everything I could get my hands on relating to the woods and waters and the wild things that inhabit them. Everything that Stewart Edward White and Charles G. Roberts wrote I read many times over.

"Anyway, these things were and are my greatest interest, almost my only interest. Now that I live in the woods I no longer find it necessary to explore them vicariously in the pages of books. Here the forest creatures are my neighbors and the countless profoundly fascinating moods and whims of the wilderness are the normal accompaniments of my everyday life."

As I fondled his four rifles with their beautifully hand-carved and inlaid stocks, the hermit showed me some of his targets which would be the envy of any marksman, and he demonstrated the opening portholes in his cabin for convenient shooting.

Looking through one of these portholes, he pointed to a patch of brush about 100 yards away and said, "A bear started bothering my

The iron pump with its carved nose.

garden. One day when he was coming in I waited until he stuck his head up, and with my 218 Bee rifle I punched a hole in his left ear. He hasn't been back since.

"The older I get the less I care for killing things. Although I have been a confirmed and inveterate gun nut since the time I was about Sally's size, if I had a son I think I would try to inspire him to take up photography instead of hunting things with a gun.

"I have growled to the people around here about the indiscriminate shooting of bears when they see them. I know a bear is pretty low down on the scale in Minnesota, but when I see a bear in the woods I begin to get pleased with myself. I like the son-of-a-gun. I don't like to see him breaking into my cabin, and when the occasion demands I will earmark him or crease his rump with a bullet, but I sure won't kill him unless I have to or unless I need a rug for my floor.

"I have criticized people for killing bears. They ask, 'What good is a bear?'

"What good a bear is depends on the individual concerned with that bear. Now, to me a bear is a lot of good. He is a part of the country that I love here. I am no hand for religion, but whatever eternal force created the country also created that bear to be here, and until that bear does something to me that I can no longer tolerate, he is just as safe with me as if he were in God's pocket.

"Now, right across the creek here is a case in point. There is a family of woodchucks. Recently I have been seeing the little young black ones playing around my woodpile. Now, to get rid of those woodchucks, all I would have to do is to crook my finger a couple of times. They are woodchucks and therefore they are 'varmints' and I don't think there is a soul around here who would say anything but, 'Kill the doggone things. They will hurt your garden.' Until that happens they are perfectly safe. I like to watch them. They sit out there on sunny mornings and comb their fur and lick themselves and have a heck of a time on top of my woodpile. It's a lot nicer to see things in the forest than to see empty woods with no life in it."

It was hard to understand why such a fine conversationalist should have withdrawn from human society. Perhaps he gave part of the answer when he said, "There is one thing that bothers me about people today. They have just about exhausted both the resources of the country and the emotional resources of the people themselves to create their mechanical monstrosities and then, instead of being satisfied and pleased with their production, they can't get away from it fast enough. They drop the whole thing during their summer vacations and head out for a few last little corners that they haven't yet ruined. And that wouldn't be so bad except that when they finally arrive at these places, what few of them there are, the first thing they think of is how to civilize them and get them like the country they just left. And that I find hard to forgive them for.

"Wherever you find a piece of clean country left like this, it is difficult to understand why it hasn't been sucked into the maelstrom years ago. There are a lot of jealous eyes on it right now that would like to see it made like every other place for fat ladies with bandanna handkerchiefs and kids with radios taking Saturday afternoon trips out from town—a hideous prospect it seems to me.

"Kids are going to be born in a few years that are going to want to know what America looked like before it was all completely under a layer of chemical gases, concrete and steel. There isn't going to be a thing that you can point to and say, 'This is approximately it.'

"Of course, I suppose there is money in converting it into available real estate. People don't ever seem to learn that money, while it's nice stuff, can cost a darn sight more than it's worth in the long run.

"There are just a few outside of me and Sally who appreciate things as they are up here. Like me, they are refugees from the 20th century who came because they didn't like the world outside. A few are fortunate in that they have womenfolk who like the same things. But this is typical bachelor country. Women in general hate such things."

As I reluctantly left my new friend and his home in the wilderness, I asked if he ever went to town. "Yes," he said, "once every couple of years if I have a bad tooth."

On the trip back to the crowded highway, towns and civilization I was undecided. Was I returning to the world of reality? Or was I leaving it in the wilderness with the Philosophical Hermit?

The carved and inlaid gun stocks made by the Hermit would bring fancy prices, but he and Sally prefer not to sell.

By Jingo, I'm Here, I'm Going to Enjoy It

Your many letters about the Philosophical Hermit we visited and wrote about last summer were much appreciated because they provided just the excuse we were looking for to pay him a second visit. Of course, boat and canoe travel to his north woods cabin in midwinter is made quite impossible by three feet of ice. However, with a map of the winter logging roads which are passable only after a solid freeze, it was possible to reach a snowshoe trail leading in to that secluded Shangri-la, the location of which still remains the Hermit's secret.

We met on the trail and he looked the same—lean and fit, but this time dressed in buckskin from his moccasins to the fur around his parka which so blended with his brown beard that you could not tell where the one began and the other left off. Trotting behind him, with snow on her inquisitive muzzle, was that little ball of animated fur named Sally. It was the beginning of two memorable days of walking his trails, snowshoeing through his woods and relaxing in the most unique of cabins while engaged in inspiring conversation.

Though his beard seemed a little more full and glossy, as if it had filled out for protection against the winter storms, he was just as I had remembered him—the same quick, effortless movements, full resonant voice, articulate manner of speech and the quickly altering facial expressions of a sensitive man.

But this time it became more apparent that while my friend was certainly a hermit, he was anything but a recluse without concern for his fellow man. His feelings seemed to be summed up in his one statement: "I used to regard myself as one of the world's foremost misanthropes, but

I have found to my considerable surprise that certain individuals I like very, very much. It is just humanity in mass that horrifies me."

Though it is miles to the nearest house, he speaks of people who live in the general area as his neighbors and said, "They are real fine people and as near as anything I have to being my friends. Our ideas differ in many ways, but they are tolerant enough to put up with my idiosyncrasies and I like them a lot. And yet, they are not so plentiful that they crowd me. It is pretty near an ideal situation from my standpoint right here on the creek. Were it not for the encroachment of civilization which I fear, I could be as happy here as anywhere for the rest of my life.

"I seem to be in love with the earth. Why, I do not know. But I have been that way since I was just a youngster. The actual things that you can see and feel of the earth are the things which appeal to me—and in their natural state, not the way we as a species change and distort them even though we think we improve them. Most of what man thinks he has improved is spoiled completely for me."

I tried to explain my pleasure and emotional fulfillment in walking through his wild woods and asked if he, who is there always, thought he enjoyed it even more.

"Well," he said, "that is hard to say. A person cannot talk about it without sounding trite. But after a good heavy snow, which covers all the timber, I like to go out about sundown and, walking down that trail, I am as near to heaven as I ever expect to be. It is something I cannot explain, but I get the feeling all over me that everything is right—just the way it is supposed to be. And I am as close to the basis of creation as I ever expect to get. It is like being in church and I get an almost holy feeling when I am out in the woods that way. The only place I am ever content or really at peace is when I am in the woods. It sounds silly, but it is the truth and consequently, when I think of the woods being filled up with a lot of noisemaking people, it is a jarring thing. If only more folks had it in them to appreciate it—to really feel something of what I feel!"

After hearing him tell about the trash he picks up in the woods and takes home to burn following the hunting season, I would now find it as sinful to drop a candy wrapper on a woods trail as on a church aisle.

I told him that a lot of people, envious people perhaps, wanted to know how he managed to lead his carefree life—what he did for money

A new carving adorned the foot of the Hermit's bed.

and how much it cost him to live there. He explained that he had some savings tucked away in the bank and that his trap line helped a good deal in providing ready cash.

"Besides," he said, "my expenses here are absolutely miniscule."

"How much?" I urged.

"Well," he said, "Sally has some high-flown ideas as to what constitutes dog food, but my tastes are simple. I eat a lot but don't need a great variety. In addition to what I grow in my garden, the food bill for Sally and me runs about $100 a year."

"One hundred dollars!" I exclaimed. "Some people spend more than that each year just for their dog food."

"Shh!" he said. "Don't let Sally hear you. She'll be biting me on the shins.

"Of course," he went on, "I buy a rifle now and then, but my clothes are simple and I make all of my own ammunition, knives, candles and the like. But my taxes keep creeping up. It seems like every time I bring in a stick of cedar, carve it and nail it on the cabin wall, taxes go up a little higher. Those tax assessor boys don't miss a bet." I about flipped

Wildlife walks along the walls in carved cupboard doors.

when he said, "You know, my taxes have run up to about $25 to $30 a year." When I told him my taxes were about forty times that much he really did flip and he said, "Good grief, you don't own a house—it owns you."

Well, by the time he got through figuring, he said, "Sally and I can live nicely—very, very nicely—on $500 a year." And from the twinkle in his eye I guessed he was doing it for considerably less.

Our hermit friend whistles a good deal and very well. Thinking of his melodious speaking voice, I said, "Do you ever sing?"

"Only when there is nobody within fourteen miles," he replied, "and I guess that's most of the time. However, when I was about 19 or 20, my mother insisted that I take voice lessons which I did for a couple of years. I decided that even if I were to become the best bass baritone in the country, I did not want to live the life of a singer."

But the Hermit does love music and listens each evening to his little battery-operated radio. Hating modern crooners and their female counterparts, he would like to listen to light classical music and asked if there were any sort of a battery-operated phonograph. I advised him that a tape recorder would be best suited to his needs and promised to fill tapes with the kind of music he wanted if he ever got one. But I didn't have the heart to tell him how much a tape recorder cost.

In the Hermit's snug cabin with its beautiful handmade furniture, carved woodwork and fur adornments, one of the most modern-looking devices is a small gas plate. In winter most cooking is done on the wood stove and he has someone bring him in a 100-pound tank of gas only once every two years. His kerosene lamp has never been lit. A trapper cannot afford the taint of kerosene on his hands or clothing, so his home-made candles provide the only source of light.

In winter, this means early to bed and late to rise and I proved my-self equal to the occasion. By the time I crawled out in the morning he was already mixing his unique pancakes which proved to be one of the high points of the visit. I never thought I would be a recipe collector, but if you want to try pancakes which are deliciously unlike anything you ever tasted before, here is the recipe.

To 1½ pints lukewarm water add 2 envelopes of dry yeast and dissolve thoroughly. Add 1 cup powdered milk and stir until dissolved. Add 3 eggs and stir briskly until liquefied. Add 3 cups flour, ¼ cup cooking oil and 1 teaspoon salt. Stir until thoroughly blended and cover kettle. Let rise in warm place until light and foamy—usually 30 to 40 minutes, stirring lightly from time to time.

My good wife has since successfully duplicated the original and I expect Hermit pancakes will be served on many special occasions at our house.

When the time came for me to return to civilization, my friend joked about my calling him the Philosophical Hermit, a title he believes he hasn't earned.

"It seems to me," he said, "that a philosophy, to amount to any-thing, should be an effective substitute for ill nature, hate, profanity, and the allied ills of man. But so far, I have been unable to make it work for me. So, for that reason, I don't think you can call my idiosyncrasies a philosophy."

Whether or not he is a philosopher, provocative thoughts are going through the mind of this sensitive 47-year-old man who says, "I think a big part of being a human is never to be satisfied with anything. When

The most magnificent candleholder. Made of hammered brass and copper and the burl of a tree.

I was a kid in school they stressed that you never be content. You were taught to set your sights on a goal which you could never hope to achieve and spend your life struggling for it. Even as a child that sounded like insanity to me. What on earth for? Why isn't it better to set your sights on something that, by a certain amount of hard work you can hope to achieve and get to it and then draw a deep sigh of relief and say, 'By jingo, I'm here. I'm going to enjoy it!' "

*   *   *   *

A Visit in October 1965

After my long land and water trip, there he stood, barefooted, arms akimbo, feather in his jaunty hat and grinning through his beard. Then that familiar, resonant baritone voice boomed a welcome across the water. Reaching for his outstretched hand and listening to the eloquence of his greeting, I was again struck by the great enigma. Here was the most articulate man I have ever met, and yet he lives away from the world—my friend, the Philosophical Hermit. With the voice of Barrymore, the vocabulary of Webster and the eloquence of Shakespeare, he has only his shaggy little dog Sally as an audience.

For most of three glorious days we walked the Hermit's woods trails and paddled his canoe across lakes and up streams. We climbed over beaver dams, looked for mink, otter and wolf tracks, ate staggering amounts of food including the abundance from his large garden, his special pancakes and cereals ground in his little hand-powered mill.

Best of all were our evenings when we sat in the candle glow and talked of everything from this world to the next. This man, I decided, fits the definition of "hermit," but he certainly is no recluse. His little radio keeps him abreast of the world. Though he has escaped civilization himself, he is much concerned with the world and what is to come of it.

"We seem to be a species that is smart as a whip," he said. "Boy, I mean that we are as smart as we can be, but we have no wisdom at all. We can think of the niftiest little gadgets and the niftiest little wheezes for doing things, but as far as over-all wisdom of how to achieve peace of mind and live in the world, the happy pleasant life, we cannot do it. Probably it's because it isn't profitable. I don't know why else. It's got to be profitable over the retail counter or it doesn't amount to a curse. We can

The Hermit makes candles—his only source of light.

do fantastic things like orbiting the earth, but we can't learn how one man can live at peace with another.

"One of the basic reasons for this, as I see it, is the actual physical crowding of people. When there were just a few people scattered around the country every one of them was more or less an asset to every other one. But when the density progresses to a certain degree above that point, then everybody is in everybody else's way and everybody is a little bit mad."

At one point in the evening, after a few minutes' silence, he said, "The world today is a heck of a poor place for me. Civilization keeps pushing in. If it crowds me here, there just isn't any place else to go. I'd like to crawl back into a history book and slam the cover. I might get a surprise, but I'd like to try it."

Then, with a soft chuckle, he added, "I'd kind of like to pick the pages. If not, it would just be my luck to hit the French Revolution wearing a pair of spats and a high silk hat."

Though frequently contemplative and sometimes pessimistic, the Hermit's sense of humor surfaces regularly and in picturesque ways, as, "The game warden was here recently but I was as innocent as an infertile egg."

Occasionally a neighbor brings visitors. This, considering his unique and beautiful log cabin, is understandable but not always appreciated by the 49-year-old hermit who described one visiting female threesome as "two embalmed librarians and a fossilized school marm."

"I told that neighbor," he said with a roaring laugh, "that I'd forgive him for that when he sent me three Viennese chorus girls."

On my last visit, it seemed that the entire interior of his log cabin and his handmade furniture were hand carved, but now there was much more—more than I could describe. The most unique was the absolute ultimate in a candlestick holder, its massive base carved from a birch burl and the intricate shade and adjustable reflector fashioned from copper inlaid with brass. Fortunately, he has no idea what some people, including me, would pay for such a work of art.

Our first dinner was an unforgettable feast. Just before eating, the Hermit picked some corn, still good after several light frosts, and as he husked a pile of large ears, our conversation went like this.

"How many are you shucking?" I asked.

"Just a dozen."

"A dozen! How many can you eat?"

"As many as necessary. It just depends on how much time a man has. Some people have talent for one thing, some for another."

At dinner I barely grabbed my fourth ear of corn before he made it his eighth.

As we gorged ourselves, the Hermit said, "This is the low point in my food supply. I just put in a $60 order for my winter grubstake. I'll entice a "leaf eater" in front of my sight to add a little protein. One deer is all I ever want. I'd rather watch them eat the cedar browse I feed them near the cabin than shoot the biggest buck in the country.

"With my garden, $10 or $12 a month buys all the food I can use plus a little dog food for Sally. If I had a million dollars I wouldn't have the slightest idea what to do with it.

"I have considered raising chickens so I could have fresh eggs and poultry," he continued, "but knowing my background, it just wouldn't work. I would soon have each chicken named. I could never kill one and would have to wait until they died of old age."

Looking at a fresh raccoon skin, I said, "I'll bet this fellow made the mistake of getting into your garden and taking one bite out of each ear of corn."

"That's it," he replied. "Doggone it, I like coons and it seems to me that everything could have been worked out better. If that coon had come and asked me, I would not only have given him corn, but cooked it for him, put salt and butter on it and held him on my lap and fed it to him."

I insisted on visiting his "Dinosaur Range" about which he had written to me, saying, "It is the wildest, most weirdly beautiful spot I have ever seen."

After paddling several miles, we turned into a bay fed by two creeks gurgling through beaver dams. Some bright-yellow leaves still clung to ash trees, others floated on the still water. Ducks and grebes swam along the shore as we sat, paddles across the gunwales, in contemplative silence. I instantly recognized this place as the "Dinosaur Range" and remembered the description in his letter.

"To stand on the old beaver dam in the early evening of a crisp October day in the hush that precedes the coming of dusk when the day wind has fallen to an occasional low sibilance in the sedge and the shadows of the spectral trees begin to lengthen perceptibly upon the dark still water, and for a little while, before taking the homeward trail, to surrender oneself wholly to the influence of whatever spirit or force it may be that pervades the place is an experience which, I believe, would haunt to the end of his days anyone at all responsive to the appeal of primeval perfection and of solitude in its quintescence. Time rolls back, the corroding centuries fall away and one looks, enthralled, upon the face of a strange young world—stark, but of incredible beauty."

The trance dissolved when the Hermit chuckled softly and said, "If you happen to see a brontosaurus raise its head, don't pay any attention. It is probably just a figment of my imagination."

That night, after we had talked and the homemade candle had flickered its golden glow in the cabin for a time, I blew it out and snuggled down in my bed as the wood stove gurgled, grunted and settled itself for the night. The pungent waxy smell of the extinguished candle in the darkness filled my head with nostalgia—a reminiscence of a small farm boy watching real candles on a Christmas tree and of cool nights in a tent. Tomorrow I must leave, but that wouldn't be so bad. The Hermit's "cure" had braced me for another round with civilization.

*   *   *   *

A Visit in July 1967

From the porch of his tidy log cabin we watched day yielding to the stillness of night. On noiseless wings a great horned owl in search of his first meal of the evening emerged from the woods, swooped upward and landed on the dead aspen tree beside the marsh. He saw us sitting and glided back into the forest.

Raising his hand to his mouth, the Hermit deftly imitated the squeaking of a mouse and the owl returned to his favorite observation perch on the dead aspen.

"A few years ago," the Hermit said, "I would have gotten my .218 rifle and shot him down. But I seem to have changed. Now, though I would like that dead tree for firewood, I let it stand because it is the favorite perch for the hawks and owls. That great horned owl up there is a

A corner of the Hermit's cabin.

vicious killer—cruel and ruthless. I have watched him kill and heard the death screams of his prey. I hate him for what he does, but not for what he is.

"It is hard to stand by and watch as a disinterested observer because I'm not. I am vitally interested in the things he kills and yet to what extent is it permissible for me to participate in altering the picture?

"I live here but one moment in history, just the blinking of an eye, and all this conflict between partridges, chipmunks, hawks and owls has been going on for God knows how many milleniums. Do I have the right to say, 'Well, I don't like you, owl, so I'm going to shoot you out of that tree in order to protect these partridges'? Every instinct says, 'Yes, that's the thing to do.' But when I stop to think about it, he has every bit as much right here as I do. It is natural to take the side of the weaker, but it is the human that seems to be the abnormality. The longer I live and

With a chisel in his expert hands, the Hermit starts a new carving.

the more I see of the natural scene the more difficult it becomes for me to assess man's status, man's place in the picture."

Again we were quiet for a long while. It grew darker until we could just see the little creek leading out to the bay of the lake and the black silhouette of the tree and the owl against the red sunset. Silence was absolute, and there was no sign that man had ever been on the scene.

At last I said, "How can you leave it?"

After another silence he replied, "I don't want to. I love it here. If it could only stay this way. But nothing stays the way it is. Civilization is crowding in and this is destroying the silence. In winter I hear chain saws, snowmobiles and trucks carrying pulpwood. When I came north I wanted to hear the wolves howl and hear the silence of things. As long as I hear civilization around me I don't get what I came for.

"Why rough it in the brush when you can get nearly as much solitude in the outskirts of some small town?"

Four times in as many years I have visited this Philosophical Hermit whose name and location must still remain his secret. I kept coming back because I thoroughly enjoyed his company. But we both knew that this was quite possibly our last visit. Though his plans are not definite, it is likely that he will move to a remote area in Canada. One place he has in

The Hermit's capacity for watermelon is unlimited.

mind is 160 miles from the nearest road and, as he put it, "I should be able to put in the rest of my time there without dislocation."

The Hermit was sad. There was the same fullness in his rich baritone voice. As always, his speech was infinitely articulate in that style reminding one of the Elizabethan Age. And at times his conversation sparkled as it always has. But inwardly, he was sad for two reasons. Civilization has encroached upon his solitude. But far more distressing was the recent passing of his little dog Sally.

Awkwardly I tried to console him by explaining that we had recently lost our Brittany spaniel, Joe. The Hermit expressed genuine surprise and deep concern, then fell silent again. He broke the silence by saying, "But you have a wife and children."

This explained that my loss was insignificant compared to his.

He is probably the most sensitive man I have ever known, and for many years his love and affection have been poured into his sole companion, the faithful, trusting little Sally. When she passed he must surely have felt that all his love and affection went with her. He was suffering the inward aches, the emptiness of a lost love.

For a year he has known that Sally soon must go. He hoped she would pass quietly in the night, but this was not his good fortune. Old age attacked Sally from within, and when the Hermit could stand her agonized cries and whimpers no longer, he knew what he had to do. He took her out and shot her through the head and cremated her on a pile of wood he readied for the purpose.

Knowing this man's kindness, sensitivity and devotion to Sally, I can visualize no more agonizing experience.

Again trying to be of some solace, I said, "Better to have loved and lost than never to have loved at all—though I can't explain why."

"This is true," he replied. "And there is a good explanation."

Then, in an eloquence of words which seemed to gush from within, he explained, "Man is an animal which must give of his love if he is to remain a whole being."

Without realizing it, he gave every reason in the world why he should have another dog, then vowed he never would.

At such times, the Hermit's emotions and extreme sensitivity override his considerable powers of reason. Like all sensitive people, he can be deeply hurt. This may well explain why he has chosen a life apart from the crush of 20th-century living.

In what sounded to me like the greatest epitaph ever bestowed upon a dog, the Hermit said,

> If, in whatever celestial dimensions she may now occupy, a dog's status is determined by the depth of the affection with which it was regarded by its boss, or by the wholehearted fulfillment of its allotted mission on earth, then Sally, if not actually Queen of the Realm, must certainly enjoy a place high on the roster of V.I.P.'s.

But the Hermit and I had our gayer hours. We walked through his immaculate garden where no stalk of corn stands an inch higher than another. The soil is rich, black and deep and produces fabulous crops of raspberries, strawberries, corn, asparagus, beans, tomatoes, squash, cabbages and much more I can't remember. I saw not a weed, but he spotted a tiny one and pulled it.

Whether pensive or jovial, the Hermit is always interesting.

With a hand scythe, he had cut quantities of marsh hay for his compost pile which could be seen steaming in fermentation in the cool of the morning. By spring it will have shrunk to one-fifth its size and be ready for the garden. It was hard to believe that a garden that far north could be so productive. He cannot possibly eat, preserve or store its yield, so much is given to settlers in the area who are less diligent gardeners.

As before, I marveled at his immaculately clean log cabin and its beautiful hand-carved furnishings. Many carvings were new since my last visit and seemed to be even better than those I had seen before.

The Hermit customarily eats only two meals a day, but after watching him stow away a breakfast, you would think he could hibernate for a week. We each had a couple of eggs and a stack of bacon, but when I gave up after three of his famous plate-sized pancakes, he was astonished, almost offended. He had just begun to eat.

One of his favorite foods, and one he cannot grow, is watermelon, so I had brought him a large one. It was worth the trip to see him stow it away.

We talked of everything from religion and evolution to the population explosion and the fate of our civilization.

Thinking again of the increase in people and noise, the Hermit in near anger said, "I don't really care a damn about the future of mankind. Mankind fundamentally is my enemy."

Of course, I know and he knows that this is not true. He constantly considers the fate of mankind and the possible effect of the population explosion which he believes will deprive the earth of its remaining spots of beauty.

He said, "People should eat the Pill like popcorn."

Still thinking of his probable move, he continued, "I hate going into the outside world again. Rip Van Winkle slept for twenty years, and I have been here for ten. But so much more has happened during my ten years than his twenty that it may be more difficult for me to go back again into the world."

As we parted, wondering if we would ever meet again, he said, "I guess I shouldn't complain. These past ten years up here have been far and away the happiest years of my life, and few men have ten years out of their lives to do exactly what they want to do."

PART IV

CAMPING IN THE WINTER WILDERNESS

The air was clear and crisp.

Alone in the Wilderness

Nature Is Lovely in White, But She Can Be Cruel, Too

Now it is dark. Sitting warm and well fed in my tent I am isolated by rapids to the south and Little Rock Falls just below me, to the north.

In a well-frozen little bay on the Canadian side of the Pine River, my 7-foot-square umbrella tent is pitched on the ice. Somewhere I had read that snow under a tent makes good insulation and, as this whole expedition is an experiment, it seemed worth a try. I tramped down the snow with my snowshoes before I erected the tent.

Bringing an aluminum tent frame along was, I am convinced, well worth the additional weight. The frame added only five pounds, and it eliminated the need for finding poles and making and driving tent stakes.

One animal I have never seen in the wild is an otter. So, while exploring the open water at the head of the falls before making camp, I was delighted to see otter tracks.

Late this afternoon while brewing a cup of tea outdoors over my little Svea stove, I kept watch over the area, hoping the animal, which looks like an oversized black mink, would appear.

Suddenly there he was, in and out of the water several times and bounding along the thin ice with that funny, humpbacked lope that reminds you of a high-speed inch worm.

I had my camera ready, but I had just taken off the telephoto lens and replaced it with a wide-angle lens to record a scene.

Well, I saw him, but unless you are willing to accept a small speck on a picture as an otter, you will have to take my word for it.

While planning this expedition, my friends thought I was stark raving mad to go alone in midwinter, but my wife was philosophical.

Little Rock Falls

"I realize there is a risk," she said, "but there is in everything. If you don't go, you might get hit by a truck on Hennepin Avenue. You have the experience to do it if anyone has, and people should enjoy reading about it."

Assembling the required equipment for midwinter camping is considerably more involved than getting ready for a picnic or even a canoe trip.

I have a great deal of respect for the north woods in winter. Nature is never more lovely than when dressed in her soft white gown. But she can be as cruel as she is beautiful. In 20-below zero temperatures, her punishment for mistakes of man or animal is far more severe than a few summer mosquito bites.

Each piece of equipment was weighed and the total was heavier than I had anticipated for winter camping. I had to include a battery of camera equipment plus enough heat and light to make it possible to do some writing at night.

Besides, I wasn't going out to discover how much I could suffer. As one of my old forestry teachers, Prof. E. J. Cheyney, used to say, "Novices

Winter woods with frosting

and Boy Scouts go into the woods to rough it. Woodsmen make it as smooth as possible."

At Grand Marais I looked up Charlie Ott and Earl Nelms, two dedicated state game wardens, and asked where I could go for a week and be assured of total solitude.

The answer would have been simple a few years ago. But since the advent of the snowmobile, fishermen riding their little mechanical ponies go almost everywhere.

Finally the wardens thought of an area with rapids and waterfalls that did not freeze in winter and portages too rough to be traversed by any machine.

It was a beautiful bright sunny morning when I drove up the Gunflint Trail. Of course, most of it has now been converted into a super-highway that reminds you of a Philadelphia turnpike, but a remaining little stretch of road winding like a true trail through the forest does its best to impart that "wilderness-bound" sensation.

Along both the North Shore and the Gunflint Trail I was amazed to see hundreds of robins. There is a very heavy crop of mountain ash

Fast Water

berries this year and apparently the bright orange-red berries were just too good for the robins to leave on their southward migration.

I left my car at a resort on the west end of Gunflint Lake. For my trek I had a little Army surplus toboggan, loaded with 100 pounds of gear and provisions.

Was this adequate to sustain life and reasonable comfort for a week alone in the wilderness? I felt sure nothing was missing, but there should have been more time to test the equipment.

Fortunately I had set up the tent at home to test the asbestos-lined stove-pipe tent hole that was contrived by Wally Clauson at Hoigaard's. The tent didn't burn, but the aluminum stove pipe, recommended by someone because it was light in weight, melted. Again I wished I had done more testing.

But it was too late now to be worrying about that. Heading north along the Canadian border, I felt a glow of anticipation unequaled since my first boyhood canoe trip.

Before long I became aware of one forgotten item—my sunglasses. But this was no problem, because I had long ago learned that tying a

bandanna handkerchief across the face close under the eyes is a good substitute.

Because the snow on the ice was not very deep, I walked at first
without snowshoes. But when I finally put them on I realized I had been
wasting a good deal of energy. I made a large bowline loop in the toboggan tow rope and put it around my waist. This lowered the center of pull
and made it possible to walk more normally erect with less effort.

Even so, the well-loaded fiber glass toboggan, 2 feet wide and 4 feet
long, did not pull over snow like a sled on ice.

After leaving Gunflint Lake and crossing Magnetic Lake, I continued
north down the Pine River.

The portage around the first rapids wound between and over great
boulders, but the miraculous little toboggan, with its canvas top protecting my gear, never rolled or slid sideways and, when I pulled hard enough,
climbed every rock.

Darkness descended shortly after 5 p.m. A week earlier there was
a full moon. Now I'll be sleeping when the moon rises later tonight.

Far from city lights or smoke, stars shine their brightest on moonless
nights. They seem to come in closer and it is easy to pass the vision test,
which is to identify the double star in the handle of the big dipper. No
northern lights tonight, just jet black sprinkled with little blue flames.

It has been a wonderful first day alone in the wilderness.

*   *   *   *

Ice Is Warm and the Stove Talks

I moved today, but not far—seven feet, to be exact. My experiment
in pitching the tent on top of snow produced negative results. With added
warmth, the snow underneath became mush, and my feet and knees made
a mountainous terrain of the tent floor. Worse, the stove gradually started
sinking and threatened to disconnect itself from the stovepipe as the snow
melted beneath it.

Then I wondered how cold it was at the surface of the ice. After
all, the water directly under the ice had to be about 32 degrees, and, as
loose snow is one of the best of insulators, why should the upper surface of
the ice be much below freezing?

A Snowshoe Trail

Poking my thermometer through the snow next to the ice surface and checking it an hour later, I found the temperature was exactly 30 degrees, even though the air temperature was below zero. I decided then and there that if my tent got intolerably cold, I would simply bury my sleeping bag under a couple of feet of snow and possibly use a section of my 3-inch stovepipe for a breathing hole.

It seems illogical to consider ice warm. But all things are relative, and 30 degrees above zero is warm on a cold night. So, using a snowshoe as a shovel, I cleared a patch of ice for the tent.

Ruffed grouse, of course, learned about the insulating value of snow long before man invented his thermometer. When temperatures are low, grouse spend most of the day, as well as the night, buried in snow. Thus preserving body heat, they reduce the demand for exessive amounts of food.

Putting boughs under the tent.

Unusually light snow for nine consecutive winters prior to this one well may be the reason for the very low grouse population. One hypothesis of current grouse research is that even though grouse survive winters with snow insufficient for burrowing, their physical condition is so rundown by spring that reproduction is drastically curtailed.

The nine winters of light snow have been as good for the deer as they may have been harmful for the grouse. I have seen few signs of deer along the lakes and rivers. This is to be expected because there is no food and only cold wind on frozen lakes.

Much of today was spent snowshoeing back into the hinterland, where I found many deer tracks and three fresh beds. The deer appear to be browsing primarily on red osier dogwood, one of their preferred winter foods. Though the snow is two or more feet deep, it is light and fluffy with no crust.

The soft snow makes snowshoeing difficult. But deer move through it easily, and they have not been forced to "yard up." If we do not have a thaw which forms a crust on the snow, there should be little deer starvation in this area again this winter.

I followed fresh tracks of one deer making long leaps. I must have startled him moments earlier. The terrain was exceedingly rough. There were great boulders with deep, deep crevices in between, but it all appeared quite smooth because of the even covering of snow. It seemed incredible that deer could run over such terrain and avoid broken legs from landing in one of the crevices. I can only guess that a deer's memory records exactly how it looked before the snow was there.

But I didn't know how it looked before the snow was there, and it occurred to me that if I were to break a leg, far from my camp, my chance of survival would be something less than that of a deer. I became extremely cautious.

My tent is heated by and most of my cooking is done on, a Mighty Midget wood-burning stove. It is my conversation piece. I not only talk about it, but to it. And it talks back. No, I am not cracking up. This particular stove has alternate illusions that it was meant to be either a blast furnace or a refrigerator. It needs talking to.

I had put considerable thought into selecting heat and light for this expedition. A gasoline stove and lantern would provide excellent light and cooking facilities, but the heat would be minimal in cold weather. Also, not being vented, a gasoline stove would not be the best thing to use in a tent at night. And besides, the amount of fuel required for a week of cold weather would be considerable.

The major factor, however, was noise. There is nothing quiet about either a gasoline stove or lantern, and one of the things I wanted was quiet.

When the little stove melted its aluminum pipe on a test run in the back yard, I didn't know that this was but the first of its pranks. Now that it has me at its mercy, I discover it has a self-adjusting damper. Just when I get an even fire going and everything adjusted exactly right, the little round damper, which is not counterbalanced, rotates by itself and shuts off all the air.

The stove's latest trick has been plugging up my spark arrester faster than I can clean it out. It started this when I fed it some green birch for which it had no taste. Now it considers the trick a fine gimmick for converting the tent into a smokehouse. It finally won the argument, and I threw the spark arrester away. However, as fire is one of the greatest dan-

Sawing a little firewood.

gers, I used my roll of aluminum foil as roofing paper. I now have probably the only tent in the country roofed with fireproof aluminum.

If you have ever been in a tent with a wood stove on a very cold, still night, you will agree that a stove can talk. It imitates birds and animals. Depending on what you feed it, the stove will chatter like a woodpecker, growl, rumble, whistle, squeal, roar or groan. In addition, a stove is an excellent ventriloquist. Several times I put my head out of the tent to search for the critter making strange noises—when they were really coming from the little stove behind me.

But, all in all, I am quite happy with my contrary little stove. When properly fed and "dampered," it keeps me quite cozy.

My choice of a light source was less wise. After ruling out gasoline because of the noise, I considered a carbide light until I realized that it required water in its little tank and probably would not accept ice as a substitute.

The stove set up in a corner of the tent. Asbestos cloth behind the pipe.

In last-minute desperation, I bought a thing called an electric camp and emergency lantern. It is much too heavy, and its efforts to be both a spotlight and a floodlight produce only a series of concentric black and light rings. Whatever I'm looking for is always hidden in one of the black circles. But everything finds some use when camping. The electric lantern makes a fine candle stand.

Fortunately, I also brought candles and cannot understand why I didn't consider them adequate in the first place. A candle is a remarkable thing. Per ounce and per cent you can't get more light. And, snuggled close in its cheery glow, I find the light adequate to read or write by. I am not sure that Edison was such a great inventor, after all.

The paucity of birds in this frigid midwinter wonderland is amazing. I heard a raven but have not seen so much as a chickadee, junco or nuthatch. Nor have I seen a ruffed grouse or a sign of one in the snow.

And this reminds me of the bill introduced in the Minnesota Legislature which would close the grouse season for two years. A noble gesture, no doubt, aimed at saving these birds from being overshot. If they are overshot, why are they as rare here—where the sound of a gun is seldom heard—as they are in heavily hunted places?

Instead of this political game management, let's help the grouse by passing a law requiring two feet of crustless snow in the north woods each winter.

Now my second day in the wilderness is over, and in the warmth of my tent I am settling down in a candle's glow to relate the "sacrifice, suffering and untold hardships of man alone against the elements."

Surely you must pity him as his story of woe unfolds—the story of poor unfortunate man surviving with no irritating jangle of a telephone, no bosses, no stacks of unanswered mail, no meetings, no conferences, no speeches, no appointments to be late for, no reason to shed his comfortable clothes or wear a tie.

There is just the endless ecstasy of prowling through the magnificent winter wilderness and absorbing the beauties of his natural environment.

There are things to do—enjoyable things such as cutting and splitting wood for the stove. There is pleasure in doing, with your own two hands, those things essential to survival, and untold satisfaction in viewing the results of your own efforts.

It is the satisfaction of the farmer contemplating his hayloft filled to capacity, or of his wife admiring her shelves stocked deep with home preserves.

This has been a day of doing, learning and enjoying—a day topped off with a large sirloin steak broiled to medium rare in a tent stove, plus homemade bread, tea and homemade cookies.

Do you suppose someone out in the world of men is feeling sorry for me here alone in the wilderness?

*　　*　　*　　*

Presence, Power of the Creator Leave Man Feeling Very Humble

I have known many outdoorsmen who have had little acquaintance with a church, but I have never known a man with a true feeling for his natural environment who was an atheist.

My friend, the Philosophical Hermit, said he felt the Power most strongly in winter in the woods particularly after a new snow. "Then," he said, "is when I am nearest my Creator." He expressed it as some supreme force totally and absolutely beyond the comprehension of man but, nevertheless, there.

This sensation is experienced not only in the wilderness. It may come while sitting beside a forest stream or leaning against a rugged oak in a wooded pasture. It may come to some in the company of others. I wouldn't know. But I think only when man is totally alone does this presence envelop him with such overwhelming power that it cannot be questioned.

Many men have felt it. Few talk about it because it almost defies expression.

Whatever the sensation, it leaves the man humble. He stands on rocks which were there millions of years before he was born and will be there millions of years later.

He looks at trees which are bigger, stronger and more beautiful than he. He may not even see the deer because they are endowed with greater speed, cunning and more acute senses. He sees plants and animals designed to live in balance and harmony within every niche of the environment—on hills, in marshes, under water, in trees, on rocks.

And overlaying all of the age, strength, cunning and grandeur that man beholds with his feeble eyes is a deep white blanket of soft purity personified.

Nothing man sees or senses on these rarest of moments leads to any feeling of human superiority. Nothing makes him feel that he is more important than the rest or that he is the chosen one. He is humble and grateful that he has been privileged to share, for a short span of years, the grandeur of the earth.

*   *   *   *

The only place I have found wildlife in abundance is in my drinking water. Melting snow is slow work so I dip water from a little pool in the river near the head of the falls. It contains numerous little water-boatmen and a variety of other aquatic life—all good protein, no doubt.

My bed is a large down-filled sleeping bag which is supposed to keep a sleeper warm at minus 20 degrees. The thermometer dropped to minus 12 degrees last night and I slept quite well, but not before I put on a suit of insulated underwear over my thermal underwear, two pairs of wool

Broiling steak on wood stove. The one candle provided the only light for this picture. (Self-timer on camera.)

socks, a cap with the earflaps down, a handwarmer at my feet and my down jacket plus all of the rest of my clothes piled on top.

(Later I learned that vigorous shaking of the down bag restored its warmth and that it should not be compressed by piling clothes over it.)

A tent has no insulation value. It doesn't really stop the wind either —it just slows it down. So, without heat, a tent gets as cold inside as out. Because the wind blew hard last night, my little stove was prodded into life a couple of times.

Today I have been conducting some experiments, which, after all, is one of the purposes of this trip. Now that I think of it, I have never explained the reason for this lone trip into the wilderness. There are two reasons. The first is completely illogical; the second—well, logical to some people.

The first is like answering the question "Why do people climb the Matterhorn?" Just because it's there, I guess. The second is to find out if

Electric lamp good only for candle stand. (Hole burned in tent is patched.)

it is possible, reasonably safe, and fun to camp out during the coldest days of the year and to figure out ways of making it more pleasant.

I hope today's experiment works because at 6 p.m. it was minus 15 degrees, clear and getting colder fast as a strong wind howled out of the north. My experiments had better work because tonight I do not have any more underwear to put on.

In spite of the aluminum sheet over asbestos on the floor of the tent where the stove stands, I noticed the stove was melting slightly into the ice. So the tent was pulled aside to let the spot freeze before insulating it with a layer of spruce and fir boughs. This looked so good that I went back over the hill and collected another armful of boughs which were sprinkled sparingly under the entire tent area.

It is already obvious this experiment is working well. While the floor of the tent is not exactly "toasty," spilled water does not freeze before I can mop it up—if I grab the sponge quickly.

A 15-foot square piece of polyethylene, which had in it an asbestos-lined stovepipe hole, was pulled over the top of the tent frame, fastened at the corners and tucked under around the sides. Thus, theoretically, it made a double-walled tent.

It may not be so good as a second pullover tent, which I had considered having made, but it has several advantages. It is transparent, lighter to carry and, most important, $25 cheaper. Of course, care must be taken to keep an opening somewhere to permit enough air to get in to be consumed by both fire and occupant.

This polyethylene is really working out quite well. In calm weather it would certainly form a double-wall tent. While a layer of heavy frost forms inside of the sheet, the tent itself remains frost-free.

Tonight, with the wind howling out of the north, the polyethylene pushes against the tent wall, nullifying the effect of a double wall but stopping the wind from blowing through the tent.

The icy wind is really screaming tonight. I have piled all of my firewood, and everything else weighty I can find, inside of the tent to keep the wind from sending it and me rolling and tumbling across the ice and down the falls. The polyethylene is rattling and crackling. I wish I had frozen some stakes into the ice to tie everything down.

On a venture such as this, one gives a lot of thought to his equipment because his life depends on it. The little wood stove with the insatiable appetite already has consumed one dead jack pine, 6 inches in diameter and 38 feet long, a small dead poplar tree and various other sticks of green and dry wood.

I had been told green pine was excellent for a night fire because it lasts so long. So I snowshoed back over the hill and "borrowed" a little jack pine from the Canadian government. I must concede this wood certainly lasts in a fire. This is because it won't burn.

To fit in the stove, my wood must be cut into about 8- or 9-inch lengths. Were I obliged to do this with an ax I could scarcely hold my own against the little stove's appetite. It is said, "Cut thy own wood and it will twice warm you." With only an ax I wouldn't even have time for the second warming.

My salvation is the little Sven saw, made in Minneapolis, which cuts speedily, weighs only a pound and folds into about half the size of a yardstick. It hangs safely on your belt.

Another cherished equipment item is the foam rubber mattress. More than two inches thick, it is designed to compact into a 10-inch roll, weighs less than half as much as an air mattress and requires no pumping or deflating. More important, it is warm and comfortable to sit, kneel or stand on. This is not true of an air mattress. For many uses it probably will replace the air mattress and is well worth the $10 investment.

It is now 10:30 p.m. and I just heard a horned owl hooting. If he is not finding more wildlife than I have seen he must be a very hungry owl.

I went outside to check the thermometer and found it had blown off into a snowdrift. Had I left it there I might have been happier because it quickly dropped to minus 20 degrees when hung up again. How that owl can sit up in his pine tree, where the wind is howling, I'll never know. I don't begrudge feeding my hungry stove tonight because it is keeping my polyethylene-wrapped tent at about 70 degrees without half trying.

Last night I learned that two suits of heavy underwear are not especially comfortable to sleep in so tonight I'll try it with one. But I'll keep my little hand warmer with me.

*   *   *   *

A Camper Can't Afford Mistakes When It Is 25 Degrees Below

I am smoking less and enjoying it more. Lighting up a smoke no longer seems to be an almost involuntary, unconscious act. I am using only about half of my carefully measured quota of tobacco, but each pipeful yields genuine pleasure and satisfaction.

With the mad busy world of man rapidly fading from memory I find myself thinking more. Whether this is good or bad I do not know, but it's fun.

Last night I had my first real feeling of apprehension. It was not fear, but stark realization of potential danger. The thermometer was falling rapidly toward minus 25 degrees. The tent was flapping in a very strong wind and Little Stove couldn't make up its mind whether to go out or burn up the tent.

However, the greatest cause for apprehension was the result of my first serious blunder. While preparing to crawl into the sack, a strong sustained blast of wind leaned the wall of the tent over the candle and I suddenly noticed a bright orange light.

Tent wrapped in polyethelene. More steam than smoke rises from the chimney at 30 degrees below zero.

Turning, I saw flames running up the side of the tent. The fire was quickly put out and the hole was easily patched with a spare handkerchief, needle and thread. But the accident was a stern reminder of how expensive a mistake can be under these circumstances.

There seemed to be no sense of embarrassment associated with my feeling of apprehension. I would have been more afraid of a feeling of overconfidence which could lead to carelessness.

When the stove settled down to a low simmer it worked admirably, keeping the tent at about the freezing point, which is comfortable for sleeping. After three hours of sleep my nose, the only exposed part, got cold. I stoked up the stove and decided that one more fueling three hours later would take me through to morning.

But even my nose got far enough into the bag to stay warm. It was starting to get light when I awoke. The stove had been out for hours and it was minus 30 degrees both inside and outside the tent.

For the first time I had a momentary wish that I were someplace else—almost anyplace else.

Fortunately, such an event had been anticipated and within reach of my bed was a pile of kindling and birch bark. Incidentally, the loose, peeling bark of paper birch, the kind you just pull off with no damage to the tree, is the best of all fire starters. It is better than paper, wax paper or lighter fluid.

With a fire going, a tent warms up as fast as it cools off without a fire, and my spirits rose with the temperature. Coffee, bacon and hotcakes completed the cure.

I like good coffee and wouldn't think of taking the instant variety even on a camping trip. Here is my recipe for making coffee:

Boil up a large pail of water with plenty of coffee in it. Without removing the grounds, set the leftover coffee in the corner of the tent. Next morning it will be frozen solid and you can take your hand ax and chop off a couple of cups for reheating. It is excellent.

My water hole had frozen over and this turned out to be a blessing. I learned that water dipped from the river after it starts down the falls contained none of the biological specimens that I had become accustomed to drinking. I should have thought of this. Bugs wouldn't spend their winter riding down falls.

Hiking through the woods today, I thought for a moment I had spotted moose tracks. On closer inspection they turned out to be tracks I had made a couple of days ago. You can't win 'em all.

Several times in the past days I thought I heard the short call of a loon, but it came from far down the river and I could not be sure. Besides, it seems ridiculous for a loon to be here at this season, though perhaps no more unusual than robins on the North Shore and the Gunflint Trail.

Today, when I returned from my hike in the woods, there he was on the pool at the head of the falls. I am camped on the Canadian side, but, of course, the loon sat on the Minnesota side.

Along the lake and on the ridges a bitter wind has been whining through the trees all day, but in the low, heavily wooded spruce and cedar bogs you could hear the wind pass overhead but not feel it. There I found more deer beds.

Even though out of the wind, it is remarkable that a deer can lie comfortably in the snow when it is minus 30 degrees. Of course, he wears a good sleeping bag. In place of the soft underfur of mink, otter and beaver, each hair of the deer is hollow, trapping dead air for insulation.

I talk too much about my stove, but it is the only companion I have with a distinct personality. I am beginning to understand its digestive system. When constantly fed tidbits, and given too much attention, it is as irresponsible as a naughty child. I have learned that it prefers to be completely stuffed once every two or three hours, have its "damper" changed and be left alone.

I am also learning about its tastes. Slightly rotten pine is its ice cream. It gobbles the pine, roaring and belching smoke. Green wood it detests.

I found a dead maple that is very hard and heavy. This the stove chortles over and chews at great length. Tonight I will learn if a belly full of this will keep it contented for four hours. If so, I shall have my sleep interrupted by only one night feeding.

Tonight will be even colder than last night. At 7 p.m. the mercury had already fallen to minus 30. I can feel and hear the rumble of the ice cracking under me as it contracts from the cold. It is an interesting sensation, but nothing to be concerned about.

In fact, nothing seems to concern me tonight. All apprehension is gone. All is peace and quiet and tranquility. There is no place I'd rather be.

Perhaps this is because last night turned out well enough after all. As with all the things we do, each bit of experience adds confidence.

More important, there is no wind tonight. No flapping tent walls or puffs of smoke from the stove. Just a calm, starlit night trying to see how cold it can get.

As man is a strongly gregarious animal, it seems a little strange that I have no desire for company. I do not miss the radio or TV.

I brought along a copy of "Lord Jim" by Joseph Conrad to read in case time dragged, but I have no desire to read it. Besides, there's too much to do. It is surprising how much time is consumed in just maintaining life and reasonable comfort under these circumstances—time cutting wood, hauling water, cooking, hiking in the woods, taking pictures and writing about it in the evening.

Possibly it is this evening writing which eliminates any feeling of loneliness. It is like talking to someone. Maybe I'm normal after all.

Solitude Does Not Bring Loneliness

This has been my most interesting day, and I pulled another boner. But my nights never seem to be dull either. So let me tell you about last night.

After improvising with a scrap of wire and a key ring, I finally induced that worthless, self-activating damper on an otherwise good stove to stand still. Loaded with dry maple, the stove settled down to a low, even heat, and I went to sleep.

About 2 a.m. there was a cold spot under my hip. As I was about to take back the nice things I had said about the excellent foam rubber mattress, I reached down to discover the spot was not only cold, but wet.

There is nothing the winter woodsman avoids more astutely than moisture in his clothes or bedding, because it destroys the insulating value.

I quickly popped out of the sleeping bag, picked up my bed and stood pondering the puddle on the floor. The tent supposedly had a waterproof floor. I was lying on a rubber mattress. Nothing should be melting on the coldest night of the year, and I have been housebroken for years.

I poked my head and flashlight out of the tent to read the thermometer—an even minus 40 degrees. I stepped on the wet spot on the floor and heard the slosh of water among the spruce boughs under the tent. Yet, on the other side of the tent my coffee and water supply had turned to ice.

In retrospect, my standing there in my underwear with my bed under my arm, blinking bewilderedly at an impossible situation, seems extremely humorous. But, on a minus-40-degree night when one is suddenly awakened at 2 a.m., neither reason nor humor seems to function very well. I threw my bed down on a dry spot and went to sleep.

With the light of morning around me and a cup of coffee inside me, it didn't take too long to figure out that the insulating value of a rubber mattress and a down sleeping bag—combined with body heat—had been sufficient to raise my 30-degree ice to something above 32 degrees. Nor did it take long to figure out that if my tent were permitted to freeze in, I would be going home without it.

After a good breakfast, my worldly possessions were hauled out of the tent and, at that temperature, it didn't take long for my puddle to turn back to ice when the tent was moved off it.

After a wet bed on a minus 40° night. Everything was hauled out and the tent moved so the ice could freeze again and be covered with boughs.

A bit disgusted, I left my gear scattered over the snow, put on my snowshoes and started up the river. Much of the open water below the rapids had frozen now, so, staying near the rocky shore, I ventured a little closer to the rapids. At one spot the ice didn't look good but, hugging the rocks, I thought I'd chance it—an error.

An instant later I was clambering out of my hole in the ice with a wet foot, an ice-caked snowshoe and a rebuking conscience.

The nearby birch consented to my peeling off a handful of its loose bark. Putting this on the ground at the bottom of a hole in the snow I had dug with my snowshoe and, covering it with a couple of handfuls of fine twigs from the top of a fallen spruce, I was, in a very few minutes, drying and toasting before a cheery fire. The temperature had risen to about minus 20 degrees, which seemed warm by comparison.

Troubles always fade quickly when I am in the woods and, as the sun rose into the clear blue sky, my spirits rose also.

I wandered for miles through the woods. Going in whatever direction something of interest attracted me, I was grateful for the little compass which has set man free—free to wander at will in unfamiliar country with assurance that he can return via the shortest route. With his compass, man has greater freedom than the wild animals, which dare not venture beyond their familiar home range.

Deer yards can be small or large. When deep, crusted snow forces all the deer to yard up, they probably occupy less than one-tenth of their normal summer range. This places a heavy strain on the edible plants within the yard, and deer so favor cedar that it is being eaten almost out of existence throughout much of the forest land in the Upper Midwest.

Here, for the first time, I saw tracks of snowshoe rabbits, properly named "varying hares"—varying because they exchange their dark coats for white ones when snow comes, and hares because they are hares, not rabbits.

Their very large feet did a much better job of keeping them on top of the snow than my snowshoes did in supporting me. The trails made by the snowshoe hares are not paths, but a line of packed spots like stepping stones for long-legged people.

In winter, snowshoes eat browse, little twigs of certain woody shrubs, as deer do, but you can always tell which one has been doing the browsing. The bunnies cut the twigs clean with their sharp teeth while the deer, lacking upper teeth, tear the twigs off with upward jerks of their heads. I think deer could well do with a set of uppers.

My week alone is nearly gone. Except for a few high-flying planes, I have not seen a sign nor heard a sound of fellow man. Yet I have not experienced one moment of loneliness. Frustration, apprehension, anger and the other emotions come and go, but not loneliness. Yet, I am quite capable of being lonely and have often been lonely in hotel rooms, on crowded streets and in big cities where not only everyone, but everything, was strange.

I wonder if we do not get lonely for things and places as much or more than we do for people. The young persons away from home for the first time may say, "I'm lonely for my mom and dad." But if that person were home and Mom and Dad went off on a vacation, the young person would miss them, but would not, I think, be lonely, because he is home where places and things are familiar.

Could loneliness be a human manifestation of that same animal instinct which causes many species to remain within their home range throughout their lives? A rabbit will run between the hunter's legs before he can be driven from his familiar home range. A quail spends his life no more than a quarter of a mile from the place he was hatched.

No doubt my analysis of loneliness is an oversimplification of a complicated emotion. But when one has spent a lot of time in the woods and has learned to love it and understand a little of it, I don't think he ever could be lonely there.

*   *   *   *

Frozen Ear Cools Going-Home Day

With another week's practice, I could learn to sleep twelve hours a night—and enjoy it.

As always happens when camping or canoeing, I again have acquired the habit of eating large breakfasts and dinners with only a cup of tea and a slice of bread with jam and peanut butter for lunch. This saves mid-day hours for doing and enjoying.

This morning, along with the usual bacon, I cooked up a package of dehydrated ham omelet which is marked "three servings." It was good, but I should have prepared two packages.

This is going-home day so, after breakfast, I broke camp and packed everything back onto the little toboggan. It took only a few minutes and I dallied awhile, taking more pictures. That is, I thought I was taking pictures, not knowing that my film had broken in the extreme cold.

Had anyone seen my trying to photograph myself on snowshoes, pulling the toboggan, he'd feel sure I had been too long alone in the woods.

After pulling the toboggan in front of some good background scenery, I would carefully backtrack over my trail and over the toboggan to leave no tell-tale marks. Then, coming around from behind, I carefully set the camera on its flimsy lightweight tripod. With everything ready, I would press the 18-second self-timer and run like mad back to the toboggan and into my towing harness—counting seconds all the way. I took several runs to make it, and the broken film makes it seem all the more ridiculous.

On the return trip I continued to be cautious, watching for bad ice and unbuckling my snowshoes so they could be kicked off wherever there was the slightest chance of breaking through.

But by the time I was within a half-mile of the end of the journey, it seemed to be all over. Hot from pulling the toboggan, I pushed my cap to the top of my head, neglecting one little precaution.

Later, I reached up and felt the lobe of my right ear. It was frozen hard and didn't feel like part of me at all.

In defense of the "stuffy" attitude of mothers and fathers, something should be said to boys who at this moment may be saying, "I'm packing off into the woods alone. If he can do it, I can, because I am younger and I am tougher."

Perhaps so, young Daniel Boone. You are probably smarter, too, and someday you may be a better woodsman. But you have not yet lived long enough to have made as many mistakes and somehow survived them.

You haven't spent eight to ten hours a day on snowshoes for five winters, cruising timber for the Forest Service. You haven't spent a mid-winter night under a balsam tree because you were foolish enough to stay out so long that you could no longer read your compass.

You haven't learned, by seeing your timber-cruising partner drop through the ice, to avoid the outside bends of rivers where the water is deep and where fast current keeps the ice thin.

Shell ice, that thin layer that forms when a stream is high and re-mains suspended when the water lowers, is something I learned about when it was 42 degrees below zero. The most welcome hand I ever grasped was that of my partner reaching out to pull me to safety.

Alone in winter, a severely sprained ankle, a frozen foot or an injured knee can be as fatal as a broken neck. You must learn extreme caution. As the old-timers say, "Never make a quick move when you are alone in the woods." You might argue that I made mistakes on this trip and came out all right. True, but you might think up a good many mistakes that I didn't make.

Of course, I cannot agree with mother's argument either when she says, "Pitch your tent in the back yard. You can suffer as much there as anywhere and be in no danger."

The yard is an excellent place to camp for a night or two in order to test your equipment and to test yourself. But there is no sense in suf-fering, if suffer you do, unless the goal is worth suffering for. A back yard offers no suitable substitute for the thrill and adventure of wilderness camping.

Camped on the river

Traveling or camping in wild country, particularly when alone or under adverse conditions, teaches many things, but most of all it teaches resourcefulness.

As a boy I used to study Horace Kephart's book, "Camping and Woodcraft," until I had it nearly memorized. However, as I recall, there was nothing in that book or in the many similar ones I have read since then, that gave answers to the myriad problems faced while camping on ice in minus-40-degree temperatures.

The number of new situations and problems that arise are endless. No one has enough experience. Possibly it is these constantly arising problems for which you must, and do, find solutions that make living in the wild an ever-new and always-gratifying experience.

A boy is old enough to go into the wilderness alone when he has attained not only woods experience, but maturity and good judgment. This could be at age 17 or it could be never.

I think there is reasonable safety in two or more mature people going into the wilderness at any season of the year, and there is reasonable safety in going alone in summer or even in early spring or late fall. But being alone and isolated in a tent when temperatures may fall to minus-30 degrees is not something I could recommend to anyone, young or old, experienced or not.

Not that it isn't fun. I found it thoroughly enjoyable, and I would be much wiser and safer doing it again. But I probably won't do it again. The midwinter woods are intolerant of mistakes, and minus-30-degree temperatures are ruthlessly unforgiving and offer too little time to correct errors.

There are many advantages in addition to safety in going into the wilderness with a companion. The load is lightened. With only the addition of a second sleeping bag and mattress, my equipment would have served two persons as well as one. The wood we cut would have heated both of us and left more time for exploring and studying the woods.

Two men can leave camp in opposite directions and be alone for hours.

But I am not convincing you, am I? Nor am I convincing myself. To attain that wonderful sensation of absolute self-reliance in wild country, you must try it alone some day—but wait until it is a little warmer.

Mrs. K. on snowshoes.

Winter With Wife in Wilderness

What have I forgotten? This kept running through my mind over and over like a broken record as we bounced along in our pickup truck loaded with two snowmobiles, snowshoes, a large sled filled with camping gear and a smaller one carrying fuel for the machines.

When camping alone in winter, I often thought how much safer and relaxed I could be with a hardy companion. Even a sprained ankle could be fatal alone on a trail in twenty-below-zero temperatures. With a partner it would be no more than an inconvenience.

This time I had a companion, but hardly the rugged, experienced type I had previously envisioned. Mrs. K. is an experienced camper and a good one, but this was her first winter trip. My responsibility seemed not less but much greater.

A camper depends on material things. Success or failure is determined by his equipment—plus resourcefulness. So what had I forgotten? What if we set up our tent in the wilderness and had no stovepipe for the wood stove? How would resourcefulness compensate for that little oversight?

But now we sat cross-legged in front of the little wood stove wolfing down our first meal in the tent—freeze-dried steak, mashed potatoes and gravy, whole kernel corn and homemade bread and all topped off with instant vanilla pudding. It was delicious and we were hungry.

The day started in International Falls with snow squeaking and crunching under rolling tires and hurrying feet in the 20-degree-below-zero temperature. Then we had driven down Highway 53 and 25 miles out the winter road into the Kabetogama Peninsula.

Map of Kabetogama Peninsula Area

So named because it is passable only in winter when the bogs and muskegs it crosses are well frozen, the winter road is maintained by the Boise Cascade Corporation for the sole purpose of supporting logging trucks which haul out the pulpwood being cut·throughout the year. But, like most of the company's property, it is open to recreation seekers.

At the last logging camp we left the truck and the road and continued some ten miles east on a trail with our snowmobiles dragging the sleds behind us. We went deep into the 108,000-acre controversial Kabetogama Peninsula which may or may not someday be the heart of Minnesota's first national park.

Except for a few months during winter, this great wild area with its forests, lakes, rivers, rock ledges and beaver flowages is accessible only by boat. Bounded on the north by Rainy Lake and on the south by Kabetogama and Namakan lakes which join Rainy Lake at Kettle Falls on the east, it is isolated from the west by extensive marshes and muskegs. There will probably never be a year-round road into the peninsula whether or not it becomes a park.

We followed an old logging road which is now a soft white ribbon of snow winding first like a deep gorge cut through a forest of dark-green spruce. Then it rose to high ground and skirted massive outcroppings of granite only to plunge again into a beaver flowage, wind around the south end of Shoepack Lake and continue its course. It was cold, of course, but, surrounded by the forest, we were protected from the wind and, dressed for it, we didn't notice the cold in this beautiful land of green and white.

When I looked back she was right behind—and loving it.

Deer use the trail too, and fresh tracks told us that a couple of them had heard us coming and had lunged off into the spruce swamp. Though the snow was belly deep for the deer, they seemed to travel with little trouble because there was no crust on the soft and fluffy snow.

Then suddenly there were three explosions in the snow not more than eight feet from me—two on the right and one on the left at about one-second intervals. Three ruffed grouse had burst from beneath the warm feathery white blanket which is their salvation on cold winter nights and days. One lit in a tree overhead, and we watched him for awhile. We examined their roosting places and found no tracks, only two holes in the snow for each bird—one where he dived in from flight and a second one two feet away with wing prints on either side where he burst out.

We left the logging road, swung south for a quarter of a mile or so to Cruiser Lake and found along its shore a dense clump of spruce, balsam and pine which promised protection from the north wind. Now the work began. Mrs. K. put on her snowshoes and started hauling and sawing wood while I shoveled snow with a snowshoe and cut brush from the spot we had selected for our tent, hoping the ground beneath the two feet of snow would be fairly level.

It takes awhile to clear a small bit of ground and cover it with a heavy layer of spruce and balsam boughs. But after that the tent went up quickly and soon the little wood stove sat in its corner where asbestos cloth protected the tent from the heat of both the stove and chimney. The spark arrester, made at home of one-eighth-inch mesh screen, sat on top of the chimney to prevent fire from above.

A handful of loose bark from a birch tree, a few twigs and a couple of Mrs. K.'s sticks made the little stove crackle and it was warm. That's the way it is with tents in winter. The moment the stove is hot the tent is warm. The moment the stove goes out the tent is as cold as outdoors.

What a welcome change to have someone else do the cooking while I went about the remaining chores.

And now it is time for me to write. The tent is snug, the wood stove chortles contentedly, our stomachs are full and the foam mattresses are laid out and covered with a heavy opened-out sleeping bag. For a cover I have an exceptionally warm down sleeping bag.

"If you want to get ready for bed, I'll cover you," I said.

Snowshoeing

Mrs. K. took off her boots, stretched out and said, "I'm ready."

She was still wearing one suit of thermal underwear, one suit of quilted underwear, wool pants, two pair of wool socks, a ski jacket with the hood over her head and a fur cap over it. No amount of persuasion would induce her to remove a stitch.

But she had her usual problem with insomnia. It always has taken her a long time to fall asleep after going to bed—sometimes up to thirty seconds.

I peered out at the thermometer which read minus 20 degrees and I remembered being told that a year ago this very week the temperature at International Falls never went above minus 30 degrees and dropped to a low of 52 degrees below zero.

Oh, well, I guess we are ready for whatever comes.

*   *   *   *

If you don't like your wife, don't take her winter camping. But if it is togetherness you want, you will get more of it winter camping than you would being trapped with her in a stuck elevator for a week.

Up here, close to the Canadian border, it gets dark before 5 p.m. in January and stays dark for about fourteen hours. A 6½-foot-square tent is not spacious for two people even for summer camping, and when you add a heating stove, wood supply, water bucket, bulky winter clothing, boots, food, cooking equipment, cameras and have drying socks, insoles and towels hanging from every wall—well, it gets mighty "cozy."

After such a long night in the congestion of a tiny tent, you are eager to be up and doing with the first rays of morning light. You are until you open the tent flap and peek out at the thermometer which reads 20 degrees below zero. Then you dive back into the down sleeping bag, chuck wood into the stove and open the drafts.

At such a time, man is justified in lying to his wife. If you say it is 20 below, the cook may be a long time in rising.

Again, it was a bright, clear day, and by midafternoon the temperature had eased up to a balmy 5 degrees below zero. It has been said by many people, including me, that after it gets down to 5 below zero it really doesn't make much difference how cold it is. But this really isn't true—at least not when you are living in a tent. At minus 5 or 10 degrees, our tent stays comfortable, but at minus 20 degrees with a slight wind, the water bucket in the corner freezes while the upper half of the tent is as hot as the top bench in a Finnish sauna.

Mrs. K. says that when she gets home she is going to give the thermostat in our house a loving pat of appreciation. After trying to maintain relatively even heat with a tiny wood stove in a tent, a thermostat becomes a marvelous invention.

Though this is her first winter trip, my "cook" is a veteran camper. Using the top of the wood stove and a one-burner gasoline stove, she produces excellent meals in record time from her compact bag of dehydrated food.

Today we cut wood and then hiked over the countryside on snowshoes. The deep, fluffy snow makes it a little tough going on webs, but the beauty of the country justifies the effort.

Traveling the lakes and old logging roads, the Kabetogama Peninsula appears mostly flat and boggy, but when you set out across country you find it rugged, rocky and beautiful with a great variety of scenery. The eastern half of the peninsula was swept by fire in 1936 so there are

Mrs. K. peeks out in the morning.

few really old trees. But thrifty young red pines are already reaching for the sky.

This is no place for bird watchers at this season of the year. We have not seen even a chickadee, nuthatch or woodpecker—only ravens "and nothing more."

I think it was Marvin Smith who told me that ravens are on the increase in this area. Well, if Smith said it I'll believe it. He is not only one of the best conservation officers, but among the most respected of men. I was pleased to learn that the people of International Falls seem to really appreciate him.

Mrs. K. learned a couple of things today. First, the north woods appears almost devoid of wildlife in the dead of winter. We saw no tracks in the high places, which is no surprise. But even in the brushy draws we saw only a few tracks of snowshoe hares, red squirrels and one deer. We did see the tracks of one fisher and noted his habit of running part-way up a tree and jumping out on the snow. But as usual on a cold, clear day in winter, we caught neither sight nor sound of a living creature other than a raven.

The other thing Mrs. K. learned was the snowshoe trap. She has walked on them for several winters but never before happened to get her webs hung up on brush and fall into deep, soft snow.

I was breaking trail and didn't notice her absence until I heard, in the distance behind me, a thrashing and whimpering that didn't resemble the sound of any animal I knew—except one.

"Need help?" I shouted.

The reply, not directed at me in particular, was unintelligible except for the word "blasted."

When I got to her, she was in the typical position of a fallen snow-shoer—feet and snowshoes hung up in the brush, face in the snow and arms pushing frantically into the bottomlessness of a deep, soft drift. Eventually one learns that the only remedy for this dilemma is to get hold of the snowshoes and pull until you get over them or they get under you.

Mrs. K. has had a problem with cold feet the past two days. I think her boots are not as well insulated as mine. I remembered that I had brought a pair of Canadian moosehide Indian moccasins to wear in the tent. She put them on over plenty of socks and now has warm feet. That is, they were warm until one foot sank deep through the snow on the margin of a lake and came up soaked. Only she could find an open spring in which to get a foot wet in this frozen country.

*   *   *   *

Who's roughing it? With our bellies full of moose steak cooked over a kitchen range, we are about to crawl into a soft bed in a cozy warm house. This day certainly wasn't planned this way, but we ran into some bad luck. Bad luck?

After snowshoeing yesterday, we decided to see the country from our snowmobiles today. We knew that a short distance from our camp on Cruiser Lake a trail led fifteen or twenty miles east to the famous Kettle Falls where two dams, one in the United States and one in Canada control the levels of Namakan and Kabetogama lakes where they empty into Rainy Lake to the north.

We left the big sled, packed emergency provisions in the small one and started up the trail in our two machines. It is fascinating country through which the trail snakes and porpoises its way back and forth, up and over a great variety of wilderness. There were many stops along the way to examine tracks, inspect beaver houses, dams and ponds and, from high places, to look across miles of forests, lakes, rivers and bays glistening under the thick blanket of new snow.

I was traveling in front and suddenly discovered I wasn't being followed. So I waited, hoping Mrs. K. would get her machine untangled from whatever she had become ensnarled with. But she didn't come. So I went back and found her sitting on her machine in the middle of the trail. It had stopped running.

I changed the spark plug and got another half mile out of it. Then it stopped for good. The engine was hopelessly flooded, and no amount of carburetor adjustment would correct the problem. So we abandoned it and rode the other machine on toward Kettle Falls where we hoped to find Charlie Williams who runs his excitingly different Kettle Falls resort in summer and tends the dams in winter.

When we drove up to the dam-tender's house there was no sign of life, no tracks in the fresh snow. Our hopes for help sank. Then the door

Ready for a day on webs.

burst open and a man who moved as quickly as one half his age, whatever that age might be, burst out of the door and walked quickly to us.

"You are Mr. and Mrs. Jim Kimball," he said.

I was flabbergasted. Few people in International Falls knew we were in the area. How could this man, isolated on the tip of the peninsula, be expecting us? To my "Yes, but how did you know?" he answered, "We call it the moccasin telegraph."

After a welcome cup of coffee and lunch, Charlie and I went back up the trail less than a mile to our disabled machine. But it hadn't changed its mind about running, so we towed it to his place and I used his radio telephone to call the experts for advice. We took off the carburetor and applied the advice, but the machine paid it no heed. Again on the radio telephone, I arranged for the pilot who was to fly Charlie's wife out from International Falls in the morning to bring a new carburetor.

So this evening we visited with the interesting Charlie Williams, ate moose steak and are about to crawl into a real bed with sheets and pillows.

*   *   *   *

This morning when the pilot, Frank Bohman, handed me the carburetor, he said, "I sell snowmobiles, a different make, but they use the same carburetor. Before you put this new one on, try pouring a little hot water on the old one."

That was all it needed. My advice to snowmobile owners is this. If your machine has a Tillotson Model HD carburetor, carry two thermos bottles of hot coffee—one for you and one for your carburetor.

In crossing one of the bays on our trip back to camp, we ran into slush ice. Snowshoers have long known about slush ice and have hated it. Snowmobilers are fast discovering the treachery of it.

When heavy snows come before the lake ice is thick, the weight of the snow depresses the ice, water rises and the slush formed on top of the ice will not freeze because of the insulating layer of snow above. It just lies there concealed under the snow waiting for an unsuspecting pair of snowshoes or a snowmobile. The slush may be a foot or more deep. A snowmobile stuck in it destroys the insulating snow cover and the whole mess can freeze into a block of ice.

Brushing teeth while wearing mittens

To avoid this trap, we followed our same trail back, but the slush had come while we slept. I saw the slightly depressed and discolored snow ahead but was too close to stop. I knew I would soon be in it. Full throttle is the only alternative. My machine with its 20-inch-wide track did well. It sloshed its way through.

Frantically I waved Mrs. K. on at top speed. She hit the slush at good speed but, its track spinning, the machine slowed and slowed. Then, just before stopping, it caught firm footing and jumped out on solid snow.

I walked back to see if Mrs. K.'s traumatic experience had put deep wrinkles in her brow. To my surprise and delight, she beamed with pride and joy. With red cheeks, sparkling eyes and a big grin, she never looked more youthful or lovely as she shouted, "I made it, I made it!"

"Did you almost get stuck?" I asked.

"Almost, maybe, but I made it."

It was a balmy zero degrees when we retired, so I decided not to feed and fight the stove all night, but let it go out. When the stove is out in a tent you don't need an indoor-outdoor thermometer. The temperature is the same on both sides of the canvas.

We slept well under the fluffy down cover, and as the temperature fell to minus 10 degrees I recall but vaguely lowering the earflaps of my cap and pulling the sleeping bag over all but my nose.

But winter nights at this latitude are longer than one can sleep. Before dawn we were awake. Fortunately, in our crowded quarters, the wood stove is only a foot from my head. The little mound of birch bark and piles of fine and medium kindling were ready, so only one hand and arm need plunge into the cold.

The fire was quickly laid and I grabbed the box of wood matches. But, alas, water had been spilled into the box and the matches were encased in a block of ice. There were more matches, of course, but they were in the bottom of a packsack in a far, cold corner of the tent. To get them meant getting out of bed and pawing through that sack in the cold dark. I rebelled, wriggling back under the cover.

But Mrs. K. came to the rescue. Now don't jump to the rash conclusion that she got up and found the dry matches. She would rather lie there till spring. She was still sleeping in her night dress of two layers of insulated and quilted underwear, shirt, socks, wool pants, ski jacket with hood and fur cap. Somewhere, in the pockets of all those clothes, she found a pack of matches and handed them to me—under the covers.

A tent is warm the minute the stove starts, and we were soon enjoying hot (genuine, not instant) coffee, bacon, a dehydrated scrambled eggs and bacon mix, toast and jam.

The sun rose in a beautiful ball of fire, but either I had my directions mixed or the sun was not rising in the east. I took a compass reading on it and was amazed to learn that the January sun up here rises about halfway between east and south. For such a short daily trip through the sky you wonder why it bothers rising at all.

Track inspection this morning revealed that during the night a deer had come within fifty feet of the tent and, curious no doubt, circled around it.

Mrs. K. ice fishing. Polyethelene curtain breaks the wind.

Cruiser Lake on which we are camped is said to be 150 feet deep and supports lake trout. While our provision of dehydrated food leaves nothing to be desired, Mrs. K. and I thought a fresh fried trout would be a welcome supplement. We had been told exactly where to fish, so this morning we buzzed up the lake on our snow sleds. We could have snowshoed, but it is so handy to throw everything you might need in the bathtublike fiber glass sled we tow and be on location in a few minutes.

For added comfort, I took the little wood stove out of the tent and brought it along. This provided heat and served well in cooking lunch, but it didn't protect us from the sharp wind.

In event of excessive cold and wind on this camping trip, I had brought a large sheet of polyethylene to wrap around the tent. This works very well as the frost forms inside the plastic cover but not in the tent. The roll of plastic, not having been used, was still in the sled.

I love to improvise for comfort's sake, so three poles were cut and three holes were chiseled part way through the ice. With the poles in place, a little water and snow packed around them froze immediately and held them firm. The polyethylene wrapped around the poles gave protection from the wind and we were very comfortable except for Mrs. K.'s feet. They were born cold. A few boughs of a nearby spruce spread on the ice for her to stand on solved that problem—much to her surprise.

We also want to report the following phenomenal experience. We were not bitten by a single mosquito, black fly or deer fly and we suffered no sunburn.

Not wanting to bother trying to keep minnows alive for a week of sub-zero weather, we didn't have any. Several people had told us that the only way to catch these lake trout was with minnows. Do you know what we discovered? They were right.

Back at camp again, I reinstalled the stove in our tent, worked up a new supply of wood and was feeling a bit disappointed about no trout for dinner when I smelled the most fragrant of all aromas emanating from the tent. I hustled over and poked my head in to see if it were true. It was. I thought we were eating entirely dehydrated food, but Mrs. K. had smuggled in a surprise package. And there it was, a huge sirloin steak sizzling in the pan. She reminded me that refrigeration is no problem on this sort of camping trip.

This is the night the wolves howled. If the whole trip were going badly instead of well, hearing the timber wolves howl would have made it all well worth while.

I have spent considerable time in wolf country, but this is the first time I have ever heard them in full chorus.

Some local sportsmen had told me that the Kabetogama Peninsula was full of wolves which should be destroyed because they were eating all the deer. Conservation officer Marvin Smith, logical as always, estimated there are ten or possibly twelve wolves on the peninsula.

Every day we looked for wolf tracks and every night we listened for their howls. We had about given up. But this evening at 4:30 when it was almost pitch dark I heard one distant deep howl and called Mrs. K. from the tent. Several wolves howled at once, and then it was quiet for a time.

Hauling wood on a snowshoe.

Then the old basso, and I can vision his muzzle pointed to the sky, started a long baleful note. The rest of the pack joined him to create a mellow and yet sinister chorus of high, medium and low voices. The wailing voices of the wildest of the wild proclaimed unchallenged domain over all animals of the wilderness—all animals except man who would shoot, trap and snare the rightful competitor for the deer he would kill for himself. I have shot many deer. I have heard the timber wolves howl but once.

Most sportsmen will claim to know the call of the wolf. Horsefeathers! The coyote (brush wolf) maybe. The timber wolf, no. Probably not more than one or two United States citizens in a million have had the spine-tingling experience of hearing a pack of timber wolves give voice. May the chance to do so never be forever denied them for the sake of the deer they eat—deer which were rightfully their source of food for thousands of years before we called them ours for sport.

*   *   *   *

It isn't that my friends question my veracity, I hope, but some said that when we returned they wanted to hear the woman's point of view. Here, dear, take the frozen pen and be a creative writer.

I did become a little apprehensive hearing "You must be crazy!" "Wow, I wouldn't do that for anything!" and "You aren't, really!" when I explained what Jim and I were planning to do—winter camp in the wilderness for a week.

Then the commiserations. "I'll think of you each night when I crawl in under my electric blanket." "Will anyone know where you are?" "I heard of a fellow who froze both his legs when his snowmobile stalled way out in the boondocks."

This is enough to make anyone apprehensive, and I was. I wasn't sure how warm I would be, although the layers of clothes I planned to wear were unbelievable. In fact, I made a preliminary test to be sure the last covering would reach around what was underneath.

The thing to remember about keeping warm in winter is that you mustn't care about appearance. To be sure, you look sort of like a blimp when fully togged out for 20-below weather, but it's better than suffering. I was never cold except for my feet before I put moccasins on. As I punched at the bulges caused by the many layers of clothing, I decided glamour would have to go by the wayside.

The only thing satisfactory for your hands are huge buckskin choppers with two pairs of home-knit wool mittens inside. Naturally you can't thread a needle or fit a puzzle together with them on, but you soon realize how warm they are if you remove them to tie a boot string or fasten your snowshoes.

It is easy enough to keep warm when snowshoeing or sawing wood. But it gets pretty chilly when riding on a snowmobile. Those frightening, gargoyle face masks are a comfort then if you can keep the eye holes in the silly things in place so you can see. Half the time I was looking through the nose hole or the mouth.

You noticed, no doubt, that I did my stint of collecting and sawing wood. That isn't very difficult and it does give you an appetite. Besides, it surely does warm you up. And when you can throw down a big heap of wood in front of the tent, it yields an ego-inflating sense of accomplishment.

I kept thinking of the Indians and the early explorers when I cooked a meal. What in the world did they eat? Here we were, with all these dandy little neat packages of beef stroganoff, steak, potatoes and all sorts of other goodies which needed only a little water added and a little heat applied to serve a pretty good meal in short order. In this day and age, with the wonderful clothing for winter wear and the delicious varied food in slim little packages—how easy for us.

To make it easier while cooking, I had the foam mattress from our bed to kneel on. The foam rubber makes a much better kneeling pad or sitting pad than the mattress that must be inflated. An air mattress is sort of tippy and wobbly and not much good except to sleep on.

The first night we bedded down the temperature was 20 below zero. Jim assured me he would tend the fire at intervals during the night. Well, there wasn't much doubt in my mind that he would sleep the sleep of the innocent and would never turn a hand. It seems I was wrong. However, I slept next to the wall of the tent which could prove to be pretty chilly. Jim was within reach of the stove. I figured that I could always shed a few clothes if I got too warm, but it is mighty hard to put clothes on in a tent at any time, let alone when you are trying to stay under cover. So

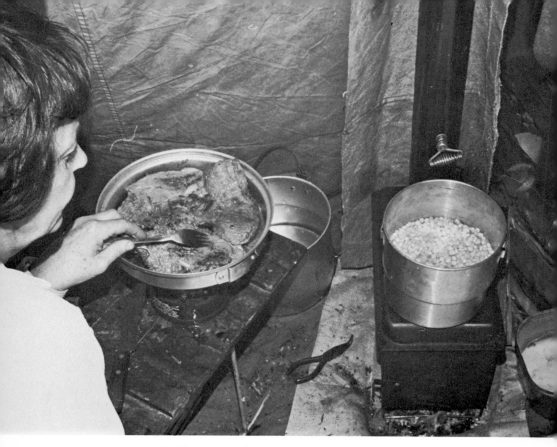

Cooking on one-burner gas stove and wood stove

who could blame me for only pulling off my boots? What with the exercise of a full day outdoors and the softness of the foam rubber mattress beneath, I slept very well indeed.

And we did spend the daylight hours outdoors. Our rides through the woods on the snowmobiles were most beautiful. The snow was very deep—waist high in some places. The trails were already made, so we could cruise along at an easy pace and absorb the loveliness of the scenery which changed at each bend of the trail. We went for miles. At times we abandoned the machines and took to the woods on snowshoes which were always with us. The snow on land and trees was undisturbed. It was a feast for the eyes.

You skeptics who shivered at the thought of our going on our expedition missed something. Thankful am I that I went along. One thing must be understood. No matter how much you enjoy being out and how willing you are to do your part, when you get to the woods it is the preparation ahead of time that means rare enjoyment or a miserable time.

Previous to our departure, there wasn't a day went by for nearly a month that Jim didn't work on some part of the equipment or write down another item on his long list of "dos." One doesn't go out on such a trip without every detail worked out. It is a "fur" piece to the nearest store.

The tent was completely assembled in the basement. Sure enough, we found some holes that needed patching.

Then the tent was set up again in the yard with the stove and asbestos cloth in place. With a hot fire going, it was discovered that a sheet of metal under the stove was needed to prevent the heat penetrating right through the asbestos cloth and burning a hole in the floor of the tent.

A spark arrester for the top of the stovepipe had to be made. The wooden box which held the camping utensils has a hinged top. When laid on its side with an improvised device for holding the cover out level, it made a fine little table with storage beneath.

So, to those who snuggled down under the electric blanket each night and felt sorry for us poor souls out there in the cold, cold, wild, wild world—I feel sorry for you. You missed something.

You see, in deciding to go along, I had some inside dope. I knew that Mr. K. enjoys his creature comforts. He doesn't like to suffer. He is no martyr and he finds no glory in experiencing hardship. On the contrary, he considers discomfort or hardship on a camping trip to be a disgrace, a goof, poor planning or lack of ingenuity and resourcefulness as problems arise. He doesn't go into the woods to rough it. Living in the woods with things running smoothly is fun.

It was a great adventure and an exhilarating experience. But let it not be forgotten that at least one of us had to know what he was doing.

*　　*　　*　　*

We seem to have proved it possible to have a happy woman on a winter camping trip—but not any woman. Of course, dear, I don't know about other women.

It is doubtful that hoards of wives will be goading their husbands into taking them winter camping. But many men, especially young men and boys, would gain much from learning the art of winter camping.

Skis, snowmobiles and light, warm clothing have taught many that winter is a great season. Why endure it when you can learn to enjoy it?

Winter camping for boys can be, with a few precautions, more safe than skiing, and it teaches preparation, caution, judgment, orderliness and resourcefulness. Winter is a great teacher because she does not pamper. She does not tolerate mistakes, indifference or absentmindedness. Her punishment is immediate and severe. Winter can be as uncompromising and cruel as she is soft and beautiful.

When a boy carelessly gets a wet foot, it is of little concern with a warm house nearby. He may do that stupid thing, or something like it, again tomorrow. But if, while the wet foot gets ever colder, he must gather fuel, build a fire and wring out and dry his freezing sock, he acquires some horse sense. A boy can argue, sulk and evoke sympathy when parents discipline him. Winter laughs, blows snow in his face, freezes tears on his cheeks and promises more of the same if he goofs again. She puts fight in his soul and teaches discipline and understanding which transcends the material things. She prepares him to cope with a relentless world which does not pamper, but rewards good judgment and lets no mistake go unpunished.

If your son and a buddy or two want to go winter camping, you will, of course, feel he is too immature. But you might give him the test. Tell him to make his plans, then turn him out in the back yard with his equipment before dinner with the agreement that he will not return to the house, regardless of what he may have forgotten, until he has finished his breakfast in the tent the following morning. If boys sleep well and parents don't, both have learned something about themselves.

There are a few logical "dont's" for any beginning winter camper. Don't start in a remote wilderness. That is like jumping out of a boat in the middle of a lake to learn to swim. Don't rely on any machine, particularly only one machine, to get you out. Have snowshoes always handy. Don't go alone. Don't skimp on planning and testing. And don't underestimate the wrath of winter.

*　　*　　*　　*

I woke up hot. My cap was off and I was half out of the covers. The water bucket which is usually frozen solid in the morning had not even a skim of ice. The temperature was zero when we went to bed and I could

Steak

not believe it had warmed to above freezing. My watch told me it was late enough to be light, but there was little light coming through the tent.

Slowly I remembered hearing snow falling on the tent as I went to sleep last night, and the mystery unfolded. I tapped one wall of the tent and a heavy layer of snow slid down, letting the light of morning enter. I opened the tent flap an inch and looked at the thermometer. It was 15 degrees above zero outside, but the insulating blanket of snow had maintained the tent temperature above 32 degrees inside. About six inches of snow had fallen and a layer clung to all sides of the tent. Light, fluffy snow is surely the best of insulators.

I'm sure I married the world champion sleeper. There she lay, clothed for minus 20 degrees temperature and under an additional four inches of down cover. She had been sleeping since I started to write the previous evening—thirteen hours.

After another eight inches of snow

The snow continued to fall during the day. The temperature fell, too, but didn't go below a balmy zero. There was no wind. The snow fell quietly from the heavens as it does in a Christmas scene. It was a Christmas scene come alive because the snow was falling, not fixed in place on paper.

Every branch of every tree and each twig of each bush supported all the snow it could hold. It was no effort for the twigs and branches. The snow was as light as the goose down in my sleeping bag. It was quiet, absolutely quiet. I wondered how many people have ever sat outdoors for an hour without once hearing the slightest sound. Not many, I decided.

This was a day for snowmobiling a little, sitting a lot and feasting one's eyes on the snow-covered beauty of wilderness in winter.

But the mind is never still, never entirely alone in the wilderness. With memories of the past and thoughts of the future, it creeps out of the wilderness at both ends and thinks of men and material things.

And so I ponder the winter purists, few in number to be sure, but purists who take to the woods on snowshoes and cross country skis. Most of them disdain the snow-sled group with their noisy, smelly machines racing through the woods and across the lakes with far too much speed and too much preoccupation with their driving to enjoy the beauty of winter.

So it is an enigma, perhaps, that Mrs. K. and I enjoy both the leisurely snowshoeing and the snowmobiling. I think they are two sports which cannot be compared. Because they are both done outdoors in winter does not make them comparable. They are as different as golf and riding a horse, but the golfer does not scorn the equestrian's sport.

There is that prevalent misconception that snowmobiles are running all over the woods disturbing the wild world. The machines can run on frozen lakes, across open fields and along old roads and trails, but this is their limit. With few exceptions, the natural woods with its brush, trees and stumps cannot be penetrated by a snowmobile.

Up here on the Kabetogama Peninsula, Boise Cascade Corporation is developing snowmobile trails as well as summer portages between the inland lakes. It is a real service to the fun-loving outdoor people.

This brings to mind the affable Art Ennis, multiple-use forester for the company, who works full time developing trails, campgrounds and other recreational opportunities on Boise Cascade lands in Minnesota. He helped us plan and get started. I smile as I remember his saying, "I'll help you in every way—except spending a winter night in a tent."

Why did they all feel that way? Everyone I told that Mrs. K. and I were going to camp out on the Kabetogama Peninsula said, "You're nuts!" The frank ones said it with their lips, the more discreet with a blank, wide-eyed stare. Could all of those people, many of them hardy outdoor souls, be wrong? And if they weren't, why were we enjoying it so much? Maybe they were right. Maybe we are nuts enough to enjoy it.

I think of Minneapolis residents reacting to news of minus 30 and 40 degree temperatures at International Falls—pitying the residents of the frigid north. Well, don't waste your pity here. These hardy northerners would not change places with you. Dressed for the reality of winter, they suffer less than you, dressed for pretty, scurrying and shivering from Dayton's to Donaldson's. These people have a great and well-deserved pride in the place they live—pride in their colorful history and heritage of rugged voyageurs, lumbermen, trappers, traders, prospectors and miners —pride, too, in their arctic winter temperatures, prospering community, hockey teams and, above all, pride in the wild unspoiled country they live in.

This explains their great concern over the possibility of a national park on the Kabetogama Peninsula. Boise Cascade opposes it, most of the business people favor it and both have their reasons.

But what the people who call the area home think is of greater concern to me. It is easy for the rest of us to say that a national park is for all the people of this nation and therefore must transcend the sentimental or selfish interest of one locality. There is truth to this, but for the people of the rest of Minnesota and the nation this would be but a place to visit while to residents of the area it is home, their back yard, the country they live in and, for some, their reason for living there.

The proposed Voyageur National Park would include a vast area of unspoiled wilderness. The Kabetogama Peninsula covers 108,000 acres and additional water and land would bring the total area to 164,000 or possibly 211,000 acres.

Unlike Yellowstone National Park, it has no geysers, bubbling pools or other natural oddities which attract the masses. It will appeal to those who appreciate unspoiled natural beauty. One cannot visit this area without wishing that many more could share his pleasure. Perhaps the national good, whatever that be, must prevail, but the wish of the local people who call this home must weigh heavily in the final decision.

The people of the area appear well divided, pro and con, about the desirability of a park, but their reasons for having or for not having a park are the same. Each camp wants to maintain the Kabetogama Peninsula as it is. Some believe a national park will bring too many people and spoil the area with overuse. They think it best left in Boise Cascade ownership for protection.

Those favoring the park point out that 44 percent of the lakeshore is now privately owned and beyond the control of the company if they wanted to control it. They believe a national park will preserve the peninsula indefinitely and prevent commercialization and the development of

Ready to go

second-rate facilities for the expanding horde of recreation seekers. So take your choice.

One thing is sure. The U. S. Park Service could gain many converts by relaxing the rigid opposition to all hunting even when big-game animals are overcrowded and starving.

Since the first day, Mrs. K. has claimed she was thoroughly enjoying this winter camping, but I wasn't quite sure until now.

We planned to break camp and go home today. This morning when Mrs. K. looked out on six inches of new snow with more coming down, she fairly beamed as she said, "We can't leave today. The winter road won't be plowed. We would never get our truck out. And we have plenty of food left."

After lunch the snow was falling ever harder. Another day or two of camping would be fun, but out on the winter road conditions could not be improving. We decided to leave. Camp was struck in a few minutes and we were off.

Instead of following the old trail, we started down the length of Cruiser Lake to join the trail farther west. With no broken trail, the deep snow rolled back like water off the bow of a boat and flooded over the top of the windshield, but the powerful machines at full throttle plowed on.

Our trip back in the snowstorm was the most beautiful of all. We poked along the trail, stopped frequently and took short walks on snowshoes. The new snowmobiles we had rented were much quieter—not quiet enough, but improved. The absolute purists may never agree, but it is possible to absorb much of nature's winter beauty while gliding slowly along a trail on a machine.

The ten-mile trip back was much too short. We drank deeply of winter's beauty as each curve and hill in the trail presented a new scene. Then we were out and one of the most memorable weeks of our lives had ended.

INDEX